Just one

biography of a Bipolar affective disorder

syndrome survivor

by David G. Keddington

war on fear, shame, and stigma. So, I'll be the first to say it: I'm Dave and I'm Bipolar.

In years past, those words would've choked me before they even crossed my mind, let alone reached my lips. Many mental illnesses are lifelong - mine included; I've spent more than fifty years with my emotions in a blender, often not caring whether I lived or died. Since surviving wasn't important to me, for so much of my life, the fact that I even still *have* one carries tremendous significance.

Unfortunately, the numbers provided by CDC (Centers for Disease Control and Prevention) tell a frightening story. In 2016 alone, approximately 23,000 lives were given willingly as an escape from mental illness. The numbers have increased, at a staggering 30% over the last twenty years.

Sadly 70% of men with bipolar die 20 years earlier than their average life expectancy - most by suicide. Eventually it's just easier to give into the voice than suffer one more day of torment. How tragic to consider that each of these men left behind a family and people who cared about them. It's just so unnecessary.

Years into my struggle, after finally receiving a diagnosis and medication, and becoming capable of controlling my decisions, thoughts, and behaviors, it haunts me to think about the people I nearly left behind. It's humbling to realize that if I'd succeeded in ending it all, the people who had shared my pain may have felt the same hopelessness that I had while holding a pistol to my head. For these, and many other reasons, I'm compelled to tell my story. It's my passion. And, it's one wild ride. Welcome aboard.

Introduction

I'm Dave, and I *am*. I'm a fighter. I'm a lover. I'm a protector, a guardian, and a justice warrior. I'm intelligent and educated. I'm a survivor, a father, a partner, and a brother. I'm Dave, and I'm crazy.

Now, do *not* take that last statement personally. I certainly don't. I'll declare it loud and proud both here and to the world. I'm mentally ill, but my strife became my purpose. And in my mind, there's no battle that's more worth fighting than one that gives the hopeless a voice. I've always taken a stand for those who couldn't fight for themselves. And now I'm ready to fight this "war" on a global scale.

The battles in this war are tough ones. But let's quit hiding mental illness. Let's talk openly about our struggles. Let's listen to people when they ask for help. Let's not look past someone who's struggling, but rather reach out with help. Let's destroy the judgement and stigma, and provide help before someone resorts to suicide.

People experiencing mental illness are strung up in a tangled mess of mental chaos; afraid to reveal themselves for fear of scrutiny and abandonment. Sure, it may sound dramatic to those of you who haven't experienced it before, but I'm here to tell you it's very real. After my diagnosis of Bipolar Disorder 1 - once a psychiatrist had given an actual *name* to what I'd been feeling for 37 years - I was shaken to my very core. I was terrified. I was officially "nuts." I was afraid to leave my home, apply for a job, attending family events, or even make friends. I had this itching paranoia that I'd make a mistake in public and my secret would be revealed. That each passing person could surely see "crazy" written on my face - as clear as if scrawled there by a sharpie after a wild party. I missed out on so much of my life because of this fear.

For those without a mental illness, it's hard, if not impossible, to understand what the mentally ill experience. Please don't minimize our illness by telling us we're just 'blue,' 'tired,' or 'confused.' We have a complex condition that's difficult to diagnose and treat. Just because you can't see it doesn't mean it's not real. It's just as real as cancer, and diabetes, and heart disease. Those diseases are discussed openly. Should mental illness be any different?

My journey, the story you're about to read, proves that a person can reach the darkest depths of hell on earth, emerge with true understanding and self-acceptance, and become successful in ways they may never have thought possible.

Chapter 1

The Cleavers got nuthin on us

My story began on a sunny Friday in Chicago, on October 22, 1965, the first male child in a family of three girls. The Beatles were on the radio, Ford had introduced its classic Mustang, and the U.S. had just entered the Vietnam conflict. It's the date the earth was created, according to Ussher chronology, going back to 4004 BC. Perhaps it's just me, but this is too coincidental not to be symbolic, and I take inspiration from knowing this little bit of history. I seek the purpose behind events; there are no mistakes in the universe. Everything, and everyone, has a unique purpose.

As far as I am concerned, the universe gave me a perfect family - a classic and idyllic 1960's household with a stable, hardworking dad, a devoted stay-at-home mom, three siblings, and a dog. From the outside, no one could have predicted that the new little addition to the family was harboring a mental illness. To that end, parts of what you're about to read might be disturbing, and I want to say up front that my behavior growing up should not be considered a negative reflection of my upbringing or my parents. There are no other humans on this earth who deserve more admiration than my mother and father.

```
        Dear Little David:


            I am almost afraid
        to write a welcome note
        to you, because I know
```

it will sound much too
sentimental for a boy.
But, I guess you will
have to forgive me this
once. You see it isn't
every day a woman has a
son. For years I have
waited for you, and I'm
certain I would never
have been really
content without you.
Nor would our family be
complete without you.

You had a name a
long time before you
had your beautiful
little body. I picked
the name out about ten

years ago and I have
been using it for you
ever since.

It would be
impossible for me to
tell you exactly how
much you already mean
to me. You are such a
sweet little guy and so
good too. You are even
more irresistible
because you are so much
like your Daddy - only
in miniature.

I'm not your only
fan either; your
Grandma adores you,

your sisters hug and
kiss you and fight over
who gets to rock you,
Daddy is proud of you,
and we all love you. I
fear you will be
terribly spoiled.

There are such
wonderful consequences
to having a son, they
tell me and I intend to
enjoy every one of
them.

I hope you will be
happy, David. I realize
no one can be happy all
the time, but I hope

your life will be
basically happy. I
would like to tell you
how to do that, but I
can't explain it. I do
know that I am happy
and you and your
sisters and especially
your daddy make me most
happy. Perhaps I can
show you how to be
happy through the years
until I can find the
words to express it.

It would please me
if you grew up loving
your Father in heaven
and understanding and

accepting His plan for you. I pray that your Father and I will be wise enough to teach you the things you need to know and true enough to live as we teach you to live.

You are so precious to us, and I'm sure you are equally as precious to your Father in heaven; we will all try and help you and love you if you will let us.

As I cuddle you close to me I feel so

fortunate to have you.
Thank you for coming
into my life and for
making me so
exceedingly happy. I
will try and make you
happy too.

Love, Mother

Chapter 2
Our Tree and the Family Nuts

My parents met during high school, and wed in 1954 in the Salt Lake City, Utah, Mormon temple (Church of Jesus Christ of Latter-Day Saints). She was 17 and he was freshly 21 and a brand-new FBI agent. Just three months into their marriage, my father was deployed to Japan (just after the Korean war). After his return, he resumed his career, and they moved to the Midwest, where they had four kids (three daughters then me) in a five-year period. Shortly after I was born, they purchased large lot and moved to the country, so that we kid could have animals and room to roam.

My mother was an incredibly strong and influential woman - a dynamic leader and educator who, during her lifetime, influenced not only me but the lives of hundreds of other children. Born in Salt Lake City, in 1936, she was a powerhouse who could just as easily make a Raggedy-Ann doll by hand as shoot lead into targets from horseback. When my sister and I were little, she went through college, ultimately earning a Master's in teaching, before starting a long and distinguished career in education - choosing posts in underserved, inner-city environments during a time when segregation was a political hot button. To place this into perspective, she had to be personally escorted in and out of the school building each day for her own safety. Her students adored her. On the side, she authored textbooks and scholarly articles. She was fierce, outspoken, took absolutely zero 'crap,' and fostered independence in us kids, exposing us to fine art and culture, as well as homemaking skills

like canning and baking. She taught *me* to cook -
the art form through which I still express myself
today. After retiring, rather than hitting the rocking
chair, she joined the volunteer ski patrol, using her
expert skiing skills to aid others. She was a
dynamo - walking or bicycling nearly every day
into her mid-seventies. Sadly, she passed away in
2017, from complications of a cruel disease -
Alzheimer's. It was incredibly hard to watch her
once brilliant mind and memory fade to a place
where she no longer evens recognized her family.
At the end, when she did speak, she was often in
another time and place with her students;
encouraging them with a smile and "I knew you
could do it!" Her legacy lives on through her
children and her students.

My father was born in Salt Lake City, Utah, in 1933. He endured a rough childhood under the thumb of an abusive alcoholic father, and lost his mother to a drunk driver (who, unbelievably, was never punished). His struggles ultimately built great character, and as mentioned earlier, he shaped a career first with the FBI, then later other forms of law enforcement. He has always been, at his core, a provider, and while I was growing up, he worked a LOT (in other works, I was left to my own devices). At the time, he was also active in the Mormon church, which has very traditional values. He expected the same of our family.

But traditional wasn't where I belonged. It was never my forte. Any time I was asked to fit into 'the box,' I'd instead kick, shake, rattle and rock it. I knew I couldn't even if I tried. Instead I did what I was good at: resistance. You name it, I fought it. But before I get into those stories, and the rifts they created between me and my mom and dad, let me introduce you to the rest of the family - my three older sisters.

Don't get me wrong. I love my sisters, but growing up we didn't relate on many levels. I yearned for a brother. It's strange, even now, to think that as the only boy, the Keddington name could so easily have died with me. The family's bets on me were in serious jeopardy as time went on.

My eldest sister has always been a bit bossy (in the best of ways) because, well, she's the oldest. Her intentions, however, were never selfish. She was actually a lot of fun, and I remember being nine or ten and dancing with her when The Hustle came out. "Do the hustle!" She was, and is, always there to support me. When I was in summer school, I stayed with her and her family. Her husband became the big brother I never had, teaching me to drive in a blue 1972 Monte Carlo. And as I grew into a big, strong, uncontrollable teenager, he was the only one able to "teach me a lesson" bare-knuckle boxing. In spite of the fact that my sister was infuriated by the bruises this caused me, I seriously *needed* to be taught a lesson. I was out of control. Together, my oldest sis and her husband raised two amazing children. She knew when to draw boundaries with me, especially if my bad behaviors were affecting her family. I don't resent her for this, rather I respect her for having the backbone to draw a line in the sand. Ironically, when her own kids were old enough to start misbehaving, she'd use me as the "heavy." She'd call me on the phone, and say,

"I'm sending these kids out to you so they can learn some manners."

Those kids were not stupid. They knew Uncle Dave was a little off balance. And guess what? It worked like a charm! Faced with the prospect of a trip to see me, or behaving for mom, they'd shape right up! I'm actually kind of honored that she thought there was something to be learned from me. And I've finally come to a point in my life where I believe she's right.

My second eldest sister is the Brainiac of the family, and ultimately became a surgeon. She was the most accepting of me as a kid and I very much looked up to her. In fact, when I was around 15 years old, I used to ride my bike 85 miles (each way) to visit her at college at Purdue University. We would walk around the campus eating pizza, talking, and laughing. She graduated high school a year early with straight A's. I remember her being in advanced calculus and physics during her Junior year and being mesmerized by the formulas on her workbook pages. As a kid, she was quiet and introspective. Nothing in the world would keep her from her studies or becoming a doctor. Thank goodness, because I ultimately turned to her for help when I was at my wits end.

My third sister, my elder by 18 months, is the animal lover and Veterinary Technician of the family. Growing up, she was the one to bring home any critter she would find. We're talking dogs, cats, gerbils, hamsters, snakes, chameleons and even horses. Sure, my dad was allergic to a lot of them, but he loved his daughter and his heart would swell when she was happy, so he gave in every single time. She has always been mellow in nature, soft spoken, and non-confrontational. But of all my sisters, she infuriated me like no other.

Chapter 3
Different, delayed, difficult, defiant, deviant, depressed, David

My own beginnings could be described, quite literally, as "wobbly." An otherwise healthy baby, my legs were turned in, and the doctors put me in leg braces. This affected my ability to crawl, and walking was also, inevitably, delayed. According to my mother's account, a rogue leg would fly left, right, left, right as I struggled across the room to reach her. I wonder now if this was a premonition of how hard I would have to work in life for things others take for granted. Hindsight is an interesting thing.

As early as I can remember, I had expansive moods, a decreased need for sleep, and distractibility, all of which had an ebb and flow. As I said a moment ago, I don't blame my parents for not knowing what they were seeing - it's easy to understand how this behavior was misidentified. I was merely viewed as a "difficult" kid. I would have times of extreme talkativeness and excessive need for stimulation, and times of dark reclusively, which I would later understand to be mania then depression. I only recently learned that my paternal grandfather (and some of his brothers) had similar behavior (bipolar can be passed genetically) and my own dad had his bouts with depression. How ironic that we were within the same walls, battling similar demons, but neither of us recognized it. Regardless, as my unidentified illness progressed, I began acquiring several other symptoms of Bipolar Disorder, like irritability, fleeting ideas, extreme goal-directed behaviors (which would often end before completion), grandiosity, and of course, the landmark - reckless behavior. These feelings and behaviors were compounded by the changing seasons - I'd grow more depressed as Fall became Winter, then perk up again during Spring - classic marks of Seasonal Affective Disorder (SAD).

One in four people will be affected by mental illness at some point in their life and eight million people die per year due to mental illness.

I was defiant as hell. One of my earliest memories, from about 3 years old, was my mother's valiant effort to give me a haircut. My first haircut; a precious milestone as far as my mother was concerned. She relished her kids' "firsts" - photographing us and documenting even the most minute details in our baby books. The sweet moment spiraled out of control when I had an epic tantrum that turned the haircut into an all-out battle. It was so bad that my mother, normally tough as nails, not only resigned as my personal stylist, but vowed never, ever, to cut my hair again. So much for a nice memory. And no, it did not make the baby book.

By age 4, my parents were looking for an outlet for my rage and pent-up energy and signed me up for swimming lessons at our local pool. It was one of the best things they ever did for me and my mental health. Luckily, I learned from some of the best lifeguards in town, who showed me that swimming could be fun. When my father walked onto the pool deck during my first lesson he was horrified; the lifeguards were grabbing me by my wrists and ankles, swinging me 'to and fro' for momentum, then tossing me out into the deep end of the pool. Mortified, he raced to the pool's edge to dive in and save me, when I popped up, grinning ear to ear, made my way to the pool's edge, and said "again, again!"

So, they tossed me in again, and again, until I was worn out and my skin was wrinkled like tissue paper. Swimming was something I was *good* at. A year later, at age 5, I began swimming competitively. In the coming years I won numerous competitions, medals, fearlessly stepped off the high dive, and regularly had my picture in the newspaper for my achievements. More importantly, swimming was good for my psyche. The pool had a sort of meditative effect on me - an escape - a temple from which I'd emerge renewed. At least for a few blissful hours.

If you're depressed, working out sounds like hell (bells and all). However, exercise is one of the top treatments for depression. We all hear how the body releases, 'happy hormones' during exercise but you won't truly believe it until you take a full breath after a workout and feel the relaxation and clarity. What about when you're manic? Do you need those happy hormones (since it seems your mind is already overdosed on them)? Absolutely. Working out while manic is a productive and

healthy way to utilize that extra
energy and still feel accomplished.
Burning up excess energy, that
could otherwise be used for
mistakes, is key.

Chapter 4
Predictably Irrational

How do you explain depression to a five-year-old? More so, how does a five-year-old identify their own depression? The honest answer to such a question is that you don't, and I didn't. I had unknowingly observed depression in my father during a few windows of time, but there's no way for a child to fathom being truly different and out of control of their lives. Deep down I *knew* I was different. And in spite of the fact that we kids were told from a young age that we could be anything, do anything, and achieve anything we set our minds to, I didn't want that. I just wanted normalcy. I wanted to fit in. I knew I had a loving home, but didn't have words for the emotional confusion in my head.

I spent the majority of my early years waging this personal war (I imagined it, literally, to be behind my face and above my throat), that no one else could see - at least not anyone around me. The science of mental illness in children was emerging, and my parents were not prepared to handle a bipolar child. They simply had to cope with my behavior, and learn as they went. I can only imagine how frustrating it must've been having a child who didn't, no couldn't, respond to discipline or rewards, but instead blazed his own destructive trail. Today we may recognize these behaviors as ADHD, anxiety, or bipolar - all highly treatable. In those days, though, help for a kid like me was not readily available.

My mother started me in Kindergarten at age 4, figuring that what had worked well for my big sisters would be good for me too. This proved to be faulty reasoning because I couldn't pay attention, let alone follow orders, and I failed miserably. But worse than this epic fail was the epic humiliation that came along with having to retake Kindergarten a year later. Especially when the teacher singled me out to the other kids, saying: "David is returning for the second time!" I had these three older sisters who were smart, good students. I didn't understand why I wasn't like them.

By age 6 I began to experience hypersensitivity. Childhood should be the best part of our lives but, looking back, I couldn't, and didn't enjoy life like the other children. Frustration and irritability would build and compound upon themselves. I would be angry with the expectations set for me, then become ill with sadness when I didn't meet them. At Christmas time, for instance, my mother asked me to put an ornament on the tree. Apparently, I didn't put it where she wanted it. She said something critical and the comment wounded me like a knife. I felt attacked and rejected, and afterward just completely withdrew (interestingly, more than 50 years later, I still dread Christmas). Like any other child, I wanted to make my parents happy and proud, but somehow, I always missed the mark. There was just no escaping the whirlpool of emotion and misunderstanding.

Those of us with bipolar disorder feel intensely and are highly attuned to how others respond or react to us. With this amplified emotional panel, sensitivity and defensiveness are unavoidable. Normal frustrations feel like WWII in a bipolar mind, leading to withdrawal, and creating distance and wedges.

By second grade I joined the Cub Scouts of America but it wasn't long before they gave me the boot for aggressive behavior. It was around this same time that I began yelling out vile swear words in my sleep. My father demanded to know where I'd learned these words, and I honestly couldn't tell him; I certainly hadn't heard them at home! That summer my friend and I stole some beer and cigarettes from his dad, and took them to the field across the road to experiment. We were seven.

Not that I was a completely rotten kid. Ever since I was young, I had a strong desire within me to serve. Helping gave me purpose and made me feel good. Not a 'manic' type of good, just wholesomely satisfied. I sang at an old folks' home, made pizzas for charity, raised money in swim a thon's, and participated in community clean-ups. My parents were proud of my work ethic - I got in there and got the job done. Along with swimming, it was one of the few things I was doing right.

Unfortunately, the same couldn't be said of school. I floated through, not really applying myself. But certain aspects of my personality - my disregard for authority, fearlessness, impulsiveness, and a strong desire to protect others - were starting to emerge. In third grade, after everyone in my class had failed a spelling test, our teacher declared we were all "stupid." I wouldn't have it. Someone needed to defend us! So, I stood up, looked her right in the eye, and loudly declared, "no, *you're* stupid." She paddled me before sending me to the Principal. He paddled me again before calling my parents. To my astonishment and horror, they sided with the teacher and the Principal! I couldn't understand how they could possibly take such a stance. A grown adult had insulted innocent children and my parents weren't standing up for us? For ME? I had never, ever, felt more abandoned. Yet somewhere deep down, the justice warrior in me knew I'd done the right thing. To this day I wouldn't take it back.

My parents bought each of us kid's exactly one bicycle. If you didn't take care of it, you were on your own. They got me a cool stingray with a banana seat, but (no surprise) I ran into a tree and wrecked it when I was only 4 years old. By age 10, I yearned for the freedom a bicycle would provide. So, I worked for months mowing lawns, and saving my allowance, and when I had enough money, I proudly purchased a brand-new bike. I rode it over to my friend's house to show it off. His big brother was there too, with a few friends. He took one look at my new bike, laughed, and made fun of it.

It was as if someone switched a flip in my head. I flew into a fury, lunged at my friend's big brother and started punching him. He couldn't hold his own against my blind rage. The other boys jumped in to rescue him. So, I took on all five. And though I was younger and smaller my indignation fueled me, and I beat them all to a pulp. A bystander ran inside and called his mother (who, not so incidentally, worked with my mother). She arrived mid-fight, came up behind me, and tried to pull me off. Not knowing it wasn't one of the boys, I threw an elbow and hit her hard in the face.

Later that night there was hell to pay. The lady had called my parents. They didn't ask for my side of the story or what had set me off. Instead, they marched me over to her house and made me apologize for punching her (automatically taking the word of the adult was painfully reminiscent of their reaction to the stupid teacher). She took no accountability for jumping into the fray. And while

I didn't expect them to condone fighting, I did feel like they could have at least *heard* my side of the story; I was defending my honor and I had never intended to hurt the lady (she brought that on herself as far as I was concerned). One thing I knew for sure - no one was trying to understand me.

"Untitled II" By Fabian
Perez, all copyrights reserved.

Nearly 30 years after the bicycle
brawl, I came across this Fabian
Perez painting, titled "Untitled II,"
in an Art Gallery in Laguna
Beach, CA. It spoke to me deeply,
and now hangs in my home. To

me, it illustrates how it feels to be
bipolar; different, alone, and
outcast, even in a crowd.
*(reprinted with permission from
the Fabian Perez organization)*

Chapter 5

Teenage boy = hard. Bipolar Teenage boy = hell

My father baptized me at the age of twelve.
As the spiritual head of our family, who held a
Priesthood position in our church, this was his
obligation and honor.   And while I wasn't
particularly interested in his religion, or baptism for
that matter, my dad desperately tried to help me
learn the scripture he believed, and conform to his
religious community and their expectations. His
church had helped him through many trials, and I
believe he thought religion could do the same for
me. But his church didn't make sense to me. I had
a bad feeling when I was there. And don't get me
wrong, even as a kid I believed in a higher power,
just not how this church was packaging it. I
avoided Sunday services any way I could, usually

by pretending to be sick, but was routinely sent by force. One Sunday I really *was* sick. But my father, now wise to my games, demanded I get into the front seat of his brand-new blue Ford LTD, for the 30-mile drive to church. We were only a few miles down the bumpy country road when I blew chunks all over the dash. Angrily, dad demanded to know why I hadn't told him I was sick.

After that, my dad quit having expectations of me, at least where church was concerned (in my head he had just given up on me in general). Unfortunately, this created a painfully empty space between us. My passions weren't his, and his weren't mine, and this unfortunate truth strained our relationship for many years to come.

There was one instance where our disagreements became personal to the point of a physical fight. It regarded my mother. This particular day, I was on turbulent waters and my mother was in the eye of the storm. To be honest, I don't remember what caused the initial argument. More than likely it was something mundane. But I lashed out at my mother, got in her face, and acidly called her "a Bitch."

My father pulled me toward him so fast my head spun. Before I even realized what was happening, he took me to the ground, and said "don't talk to my wife like that." I had crossed a boundary and we both knew it. My dad is not a large man. I was a full head taller, 30 lbs. heavier, and very fit from swim racing, but he took me out swiftly. It was a good lesson in respect, and I never crossed that line again. And while physical altercation isn't a recommended method for handling problems, there are some times that you must stand up for yourself or a loved one. I'm grateful he protected his wife (my mother), and me from my darker self. I needed saving and warnings could only go so far.

This isn't to say my father hadn't tried to meet me on the same page. But with our dissimilar interests, and his demanding work and church volunteer schedule, we had very little time together. He'd drop me off at my 6:00 a.m. swim practice, and sometimes pick me up at the end of a long day, but we weren't connecting on an emotional level. I honestly don't know if I could have, even if I'd wanted to.

What he didn't know, no one knew, was that I was now hearing a voice in my head that told me to kill myself. Sometimes the voice came to me once or twice a day. But other times, it was there ALL the time - tormenting me, saying "you should just go kill yourself. You're no good. You're not worth it." Sometimes for months at a time. To make things worse, I couldn't tell anyone! No one had listened in the past. And my dad's religion said suicide was a mortal sin, and that if I followed through, I'd be condemned to hell. How does a 12-year-old boy bring that up to his mom and dad?

Life with bipolar affective disorder is like living life in stanzas. Imagine a playlist of your favorite and most hated songs. Your favorite songs make you feel

strong. Powerful. Unstoppable.
But imagine NOT being in control
of your playlist, and the tune
changing to one you HATE, and
that song blaring in your head
24/7, and it's impossible to block
out. Would it drive you crazy?
That's the "voice" I described.
It's tormenting and unrelenting.
Some days that's how it feels to be
bipolar.

I isolated myself and started to self-mutilate
with a razor blade. I didn't know what else to do.
I wanted the torment to end. When it got to be too
much, I grabbed the sharp blade and slowly,
meticulously, sliced open the outside of my
forearms until they bled. It was such a relief, both

physically and mentally, to see and feel the warm, thick, liquid running down my arms. The voice would stop. And while I knew my behavior wasn't "normal," I really didn't care. It was a way I could relieve and give physical form to my inner pain without killing myself - documentation of the emotions I couldn't otherwise articulate. No one had taught me or influenced me - the self-mutilations were part of a punishment I'd designed for myself. I'd hide my deed by wearing long-sleeved shirts and telling elaborate lies. I soothed myself this way into my early twenties, at which point I switched from a blade to a bottle of Jack Daniels.

When I was cutting, I thought I was the only one. But in actuality, self-mutilation is as old as time.

The ancient Greek historian, Herodotus, wrote of a Spartan leader who was placed in the stocks for abnormal behaviors. When given a knife, he went to work slicing away at his shins and thighs. The point is, these aren't modern issues. These are people issues. We need to eliminate the shame, realize some people are desperate (most of us, after all, spend our lives *avoiding* pain), and see it for what it really is - a cry for help.

I expressed through cutting. But self-mutilation can take many other forms, including burning, biting, hair pulling, nail biting, scratching, intentional bruising, pulling scabs, ripping scars, slapping, and even burning with acid. The mind is most creative when desperate.

Alcohol was becoming a bigger part of my life and by age 14 was my preferred method of self-medication. Left to my own devices, I'd steal beer from our neighbors' garage refrigerators. At the time I considered it partying, but looking back, I can see that I was self-medicating. Dad caught me with a bottle of peach schnapps once, but I played it off as an isolated incident. He and my mother had no idea how much I was *really* drinking, or how dependent I was becoming.

Increasingly irrational, I would snap with rage when I felt frustrated. Once, when I was 13 and my sister was 15, I found myself holding a knife to her throat over the use of the telephone. It was one of the scariest moments of my life and it makes me sick now to even think about it. I harbor no guilt, because I know I love my sister and I understand my illness, but it goes to show how much a bipolar mood swing can cause a person to deviate from their true character, and how dangerous my disease was becoming.

At this point you may be wondering why no one noticed and intervened. While I'm not busting their chops, my family knew something was wrong (my oldest sister says she knew I was "off" by the time I was 10), and my dad admits now that he didn't think I'd live to see age 30. But in those days, the stigma of having a family member with a mental illness was incredibly strong. It was an embarrassment, an admission of failure, and a stain on the family. I don't think they knew what to do with me, so they did nothing, and hoped it would go away. The hell I put them through, with my isolation, unpredictability, and sometimes explosive nature, is still hard for me to reconcile. Obviously, I can't go back and change things, but in hindsight I wish that *they* would have had someone to talk to. Someone who could relate to what they were going through. Someone to make sense of the chaos that was their son.

Chapter 6
Papa tried

In spite of our prior troubles (and what my head was telling me), my dad wasn't giving up on me. To bring us closer together, he took me to the lake and got us a rowboat with a tiny, three-horsepower motor. We carried the rig to the water and set out on our father-son excursion.

True to the recurring force in our relationship, things swiftly fell apart. Once afloat we went to start the motor, but it wouldn't work. Unbeknownst to us, the propeller and shaft had fallen off into the water and sunk to the bottom of the lake. We were adrift. And I can't help but see the symbolism in that! I felt terrible for my dad; my heart broke for him. He had put forth such effort to create a memory with me and it all went sideways. The graceful man he is, he didn't scream, yell or swear. He just took a deep breath and devised a plan to get us to shore. We rowed ourselves into the bay and left the beautiful attempt without any discussion. I gained a timeless memory regardless of how the events played out. If anything, I hold it closer, and place more value in it, because it *didn't* play out perfectly. I knew my dad loved me.

His efforts toward mutual understanding didn't stop there. He took me on another fishing trip (this time to Canada) and again, we ended up in a boat knowing about as little as we had before. We didn't catch a single fish for the first couple of days until a kind local man took pity and taught us the tricks of the trade. Luckily this time the motor stayed on the boat. But dad got too close to the edge, lost his balance, and fell into the frigid water. Surprisingly (thankfully), he emerged with a sheepish ear-to-ear smile and a big hearty laugh. The laugh was, for us, strangely healing. We continued laughing even after he was back in the boat and warming up. Fishermen are intended to stay *in* the boat, and the fish in the water (at least until you catch 'em), and teenage boys are supposed to be "normal" but sometimes they aren't. Apparently, we Keddington men enjoy doing things the hard way. The best part about this adventure was enjoying each other's company, learning, relaxing, laughing, and just really finding common ground. It's a sacred memory I treasure; one I'll never forget.

Swimming continued to be an outlet for my pent-up confusion and anger and helped to keep me level emotionally. I competed on the club level during the summers, attending practices twice a day, and was a dedicated team member. This served the team, but in reality, it served me. What I couldn't tell anyone was that when I was in the pool, swimming laps for hours at a time, the voice was quiet and I had a momentary break from the unrelenting torment. Swimming literally saved me from myself.

My first paid job was baling hay for a farmer at age fourteen. I'd ride my bike seven miles to the farm, and work alongside the owner and his son (a lanky blonde with a farmer's tan), earning $2.85 per hour plus lunch. It was hard work and I was good and tired by the end of the day. During this time the cutting subsided. With all of the nonstop physical activity, and the distraction of having to pay attention to the machinery, I had a brief period of peace.

Between farming and swimming, I grew lean and muscular, which attracted the attention of a few local girls. Let's be honest - I was a teenage boy and I didn't mind! Yet I had been raised to be respectful of women (strong mother and three older sisters, remember?), so I was nice, and the girls liked me. While the other boys were cat-calling and acting immature and rude, I spent the summer hanging out with these girls - talking, going to movies, and playing basketball and tennis. Meanwhile, I kept up a good front for my friends' parents. Because I acted so politely, they all thought I was an angel. This was, of course, a total facade. Behind the scenes I was drinking, fighting, finding trouble, and my sanity was in a rapid decline.

Chapter 7

I'm in the Tunnel - where's the light?

High school was a struggle for me. I had disdain for the authoritarian style of the educational system and how they treat non-conformity, or what I preferred to call 'originality'. I had all I could do to maintain a socially acceptable persona. Academically, I had no interest in applying myself and barely earned C's - the minimum required to stay on the swim team. To complicate matters, my mother taught at the school, and my father was on the school board. People knew our family; it wasn't like I could fly under the radar.

My temper was hot, and more unpredictable than ever. This, coupled with the fact that I was now 6'1" tall, 180 lbs., extremely fit, disliked authority, and never backed down from a fight, made for a toxic combination.

Freshman year, when my football coach said something rude and demeaning, I punched him right in the face. After that, the school Athletic Director limited me to individual, non-contact sports. I think the only reason I got to stay in sports at all was as a professional courtesy to my parents.

Mental illness isn't invisible to the naked eye like many of us believe. There are so many signs and indications of when someone you love could need help. If you see something, don't turn a blind eye. Start asking questions. Don't think of it as interfering in something that isn't your business. Think of it as potentially saving a life.

Not long after that, my Algebra teacher accused me of cheating (I wasn't - the guy next to me was a worse student than I). I made a snide comment, and the teacher got up and moved toward me quickly. Without hesitation, I stood up, spun around, and punched him in the gut so hard that he doubled over. I showed myself to the Principal's office and announced my crime. By then I was a regular.

And remember that Principal from third grade? The one who paddled me? One day I saw him in the pool locker room at my school. My turf. I walked up to him, smiled, and said "if I ever see you outside of here, we're going to have a problem." Compared to me now, he was puny. He stared at me with wide eyes and didn't utter a word. Not a word. Funny stuff. I like to think it helped him understand that he should be nicer to little kids.

My aggression wasn't always a bad thing. Sometimes I used it for good. My mother taught a Resource class (for the mentally disabled kids). I had that period free, so I'd help in her class, and got to know and like the kids. When I saw them being bullied in the hall (which, unfortunately, was not uncommon), the protector and justice warrior surfaced, and bashed more than a few heads into lockers. F-ing assholes.

Because I was such a loose cannon, mistrust still lingered under the surface where my parents were concerned. One winter afternoon, my dad took me down to the local police station and walked me into an interrogation room with a police officer.

"Where'd you hide it?" the officer asked.

"Hide what?" I answered, completely bewildered.

"The snowmobile," she answered.

"What snowmobile? What the hell are you talking about" I said.

I honestly had no idea what she was talking about, but this idiot had herself convinced (and my dad, apparently, too) that I was the culprit in the case of the stolen snowmobile. My dad sat there, looking disappointed. There was zip zero benefit-of-the-doubt for Dave, just this general assumption that because I was finding trouble elsewhere, that I must be behind this crime too. I didn't hear if they ever solved that crime. The only thing resolved that day was in my own head. Why even try? I was going to be accused anyway.

Swimming was the only high point, the one good thing in my life, and the only thing I looked forward to. I was a sprinter, and raced Freestyle and Butterfly, breaking school records and placing at the state tournament. Outside of school, I was drinking every day, stealing my mom's car to go on joyrides, and generally raising hell. In time, I discovered girls, and started having sex (sometimes protected, sometimes not), without a second thought to the risks I was taking. I honestly didn't care about consequences to ANY of my actions. I was adrift with no direction or purpose.

Chapter 8

The Bridge Between Reality and My Future

But all that changed at the end of my Sophomore year when I met a military recruiter who sold me on a life of service. Service and protection were part of my DNA. It seemed a perfect recipe for happiness and success, and interestingly, the standards of the military were ones I could accept. They had a rulebook to life, per se. They laid out EXACTLY what you could and couldn't do, they taught you a job, then expected you excel at it. I loved the idea of this structure, and I thought their regulations could fix me. I mean, how could I screw up at something so organized and precise?

I made up my mind. I had never been so sure about anything. My parents signed the consent papers, and shortly afterward, at age 16, with the recruiter standing over my shoulder, I confidently drug my pen across parchment, making myself the future legal property of the U.S. government. I couldn't wait to move forward, get out of my hometown, and start my new life.

But there was *one* small hitch. The military required that I graduate before I signed on. That meant making up for lost time and missed classes. Although it may sound strange, a switch flipped in my head, and, with the military as my goal, I approached school with a vigor. Not only did I have to pass each class (mediocrity isn't in the military Bible), but I also had to earn a solid grade to meet the entry qualifications. I accelerated my studies, taking night school and summer school, working harder on my academics than ever before, to catch up and build a bridge between my high school life and my adult life. My successes were fueling my drive and I was not ready to let this control slide from my fingers. In August of 1983, at the age of 17, the former D student graduated, with A's and B's (get this) an *entire YEAR early!* Because it was summer, I didn't have a graduation ceremony. That was just fine with me.

The shackles were off. I was set to swear in on Sept 19, which meant I had about one month of freedom before making my formal transition to adulthood. My parents, delighted at my turn-around, offered to pay for a senior trip. So, my best friend and I hopped a train to southern California to spend a few weeks at the beach. It was a real adventure. We laughed, drank beer, and smoked clove cigarettes with other travelers, at night sleeping in the baggage compartment on top of our luggage.

Once to California, we hitchhiked to Laguna Beach, where we swam in the ocean, bummed around, and slept on the beach under a house on piers. It was so, so peaceful, and, to this point, the happiest moment of my life. I was free, on an adventure with my best friend, and there was nobody around to tell us what to do.

That night, in our sleeping bags under the pier, we watched five teenagers strip bare naked and run into the water for a moonlight swim. They were being exceptionally loud, which woke up the elderly inhabitant of the beach house (directly above our heads). In an act of revenge, he walked down the creaky wooden steps, right above where my friend and I were hidden, picked up every single bit of the teenager's clothing, and took everything into his house. When the rowdy group came out of the water, cold and naked, and couldn't find their clothes, they had no clue what to do. We watched the whole scene played out before our eyes and laughed for hours, not because of the humiliation, but because if it had been another place and time that would have been us. I wouldn't trade that memory for the world.

My parents flew in from the Midwest to join us for a couple of days. We lunched and spent the day with them by the ocean, celebrating my grand farewell. It had been a rough road for ALL of us, and I think they were relieved to see that I was turning my life around. A few days later, my friend and I hopped the train back east, stopping in Utah to camp and hike in the mountains. We pitched our tents next to a lake, near the top of a peak, at a ski resort.

We'd had a rough time getting there. The trails were wide and steep, and, true to my nature, I had picked the one of toughest routes up. It took what felt like FOREVER to get there. When we did finally reach the lake, between gasps of breath I declared, "this is where we set up camp." The sight, at 9,800 feet, next to the crystal-clear lake, was nothing short of spectacular. Even though it was late summer the water in the lake was nearly freezing.

As we set up and hammocks and camp, the sun was going down, fast, over the mountains, and I decided to have a little fun hassling my friend (a novice to mountain camping).

"You better get in your hammock before the critters come out," I told him.

Completely startled, he hopped up to his hammock, missed, flipped it over, and ejected out the other side, rolling down the hill right into the frigid lake. It was hysterical (okay - maybe not to him). After contacting the nearly freezing water, then jumping out into the brisk mountain air, his survival instincts kicked in, and he stripped like the frantic streake'rs of Laguna Beach. He spent the night wrapped in just his dry, warm sleeping bag.

Once he was over being mad at me, we laughed for hours, and slept the best we had in weeks.

The next day we packed up and began making our way down the mountain on cat tracks (used during the winter season to get grooming machinery to the top of the mountain). Again, it was tough going; our feet became blistered, and my friend, who was not in shape like me, was cursing me and trailing behind. Eventually, a man came along in a truck and asked me if we wanted a ride. Before my friend could get there, I dismissed the offer. When he caught up, and found out I'd sent our ride away, he was red-face livid. These are the types of nonsensical decisions made while riding a manic high. I didn't realize it at the time, but intentionally inflicting pain on a friend, to prove a point, isn't much different than the harm I did with my blade back home.

My friend forgave me (again), and we made our way back home. In many ways the trip defined who I was. There was liberation in knowing 'quit' wasn't an option for me. I could graduate, I could look after myself, and I could physically conquer what I put my mind to. It was the perfect preface to the next stage of my life.

Chapter 9
Building a Warrior

A few weeks later, I formally entered the United States Army. My basic combat training took place in Ft. Jackson, South Carolina. Turning a civilian into a soldier isn't a simple, pleasant or quick process. The new troops are wiped nearly clean of the lives they led before joining. I was okay with that, since I was doing *exactly* what I wanted. I hoped to forget my old life, cleanse myself, and have a new beginning. For nine weeks the core values of loyalty, duty, respect, selflessness, honor, integrity, and courage were drilled so far into me, I started to believe it like it was Gospel.

There's a term used to describe week one and it is 'TOTAL CONTROL.' You do what your Drill Sergeant says and *nothing* else. Every misstep can lead to a 'drop,' which is short for 'drop and give me twenty.' This doesn't seem so harsh until you've 'dropped' twenty times. Their method of control was hard discipline and fine lines that could not be crossed. Because I knew, somewhere deep down, that I wasn't 'right' in the head, I thought I needed someone to control me (just as I had needed my father to show me the lines as a teenager). The days started bright and early, at 0430, so that as soldiers, we would 'complete more before 9 a.m. than most do in their entire day.' Make yourself useful and, most importantly, make yourself productive. And that's what I did. I took physical training to the next level and burned off a lot of the angst I had been feeling for the majority of my life.

The military removes the term 'why' from your vocabulary; I didn't have a need for it. I wanted direction. I wanted precision. I wanted the consistency that I couldn't give to myself. However, I could have done without the tear C.S. (tear) gas chamber. You're exposed to C.S. gas in training to prove you've really got what it takes. But I had been breathing in hairspray from my sisters for years. I had that on lockdown.

You may find it odd that Dave, the rebel, liked this structure. The best way I can explain this is to say that, in the Army, it was hard to get in trouble. The rules were defined and all I had to do was follow them. To me the structure was a strangely freeing. It gave me a purpose and it made me strive to do better.

The way in which the military handled mental illness when I was a soldier can be summed up in three words. Not. At. All. (it bears noting that circ. 2019 this has improved greatly, but there's still a long way to go). Unseen and unheard equaled not real. Ever heard of 'don't ask, don't tell?' Well it applies to more oppressed groups than the LGBTQ community. What most civilians don't understand is that there are professional consequences to coming forward to ask for help with mental illness. In fact, a soldier can be dishonorably discharged, which is more than a stain on their name. Dishonorable discharge means that benefits and future civilian employment are compromised. That's part of the reason we see homeless, ill, veterans roaming the streets, and it breaks my heart. Had circumstances been any different, this easily could've been me.

After basic training I was shipped off on a bus to Ft. Gordon, Georgia to begin my classroom training for my Military Occupational Specialty (MOS) training in communications. My platoon and I formed a cohesive group. A brotherhood. There wasn't anything I could have said or done to make myself unfit for these new brothers and, importantly, it was the first time that I had ever experienced complete acceptance. Unlike basic training, we were allowed to pick a physical activity we liked. I chose boxing and began training regularly. And since I had a bit of a (ahem) "history," I excelled.

Day to day banter among soldiers would be considered unacceptable by regular societal standards. We spoke offensively for fun;

conversations and jokes about death and violence were the norm. Maybe it's understandable considering what a soldier is trained for. Maybe it's a way to normalize the violence - especially when you consider yourselves the "good guys."

With this mindset, it wasn't uncommon that a few brothers and I would go into town, off duty, get loaded on whiskey at a bar, then start a fight "just for the fun of it." We became somewhat legendary after a few of these brawls, earning the name "The Wrecking Crew." More than once we ended up in jail but there were never any long-term repercussions.

After three months of boxing, bookwork (where I learned Microwave Multi-channel Communications), and general misbehavior, I was

ready for the real excitement. Jump School!
Once again, I shipped out - this time to Ft.
Benning, Georgia. Jump school was another
opportunity to propel me forward in the ranks. Our
class was led by a "Black Hat" known as Sergeant
Airborne, who used the 'tough love' method of
teaching. Granted, it was for the trainee's
wellbeing, so it wasn't personal (most of the time).
There was a lot of physical demand in the military,
in general, but jump school laid it on hard. We ran
everywhere in formation, in combat boots, carrying
up to 70 pounds of equipment. We also learned the
Parachute Landing Fall (PLF). I must not have
paid close enough attention, because that's where I
ultimately came up short.

It happened on my third jump. To this day,
I'm not even sure what exactly went wrong. But I

landed incorrectly, shattering the end of my femur (the medial femoral condyle, to be exact), effectively 'blowing out' my right knee. At that moment, all I could hear was a loud pop, then a crack. The biggest trouble wasn't with the broken bone though. It was the grueling 5 mile run back to the barracks. The most painful part of the run wasn't my destroyed leg. It was my destroyed pride.

Need I remind you how hard I had worked to qualify for the military, or my passion for service, or how important this was for my pride and mental health? My desperate desire to fulfill my dream took over. I wasn't ready to give up and this drive gave me the fuel I needed to push through the excruciating pain and move forward. So instead of telling anyone what had happened I picked myself up, brushed myself off, and did my best to run without drawing notice to myself. You see, if they caught wind of my injury, they would pull me out, and I'd lose everything I'd worked for. I ran in the rear of the formation, with the Captain, to stay under the radar and keep pace. Before long, my right leg folded beneath me, sending me into a somersault. The Captain halted and asked me what was going on. Numbed by the pain and shock (the memory is a bit of a blur), I remember telling him that I had tripped, and there was nothing else to it. Miraculously, he believed me. It's not the only time in my life that fate allowed me to slip through the cracks.

The problem was, this injury wasn't one that could be hidden long term. My secret wouldn't be a secret forever, but I rode it out as long as possible.

I finished two more jumps even through moments where my leg would lock up like a metal rod (due to silver-dollar-sized shards of bone hindering the movement of my joint). Walking created crunching sounds and my muscles seemed to squeak around the inflamed knee. I honestly don't know how I even stood up. No, actually, I do. The mind is a powerful thing. And with enough heart to back it up, a person can do nearly anything.

After jump school, I received really disappointing news. When I'd signed on a year earlier, the Army had asked where I'd like to go after training. Preferring a cooler climate, I put in for Germany, Alaska, and Japan. So, where did the Army send me? Panama. Yep, tropical jungle, stifling heat, high humidity, bugs and snakes Panama. That one. Central America. Hooray.

My first official job in the Army wasn't nearly as glorified as the picture I had painted in my head. At that time there was political unrest in Panama - so much so that American troops had all moved from their bases into the jungle. I was tasked with marching in front of a slow-moving jeep, as it made its way through the dense jungle, to make sure there were no hazards or obstructions in its path. I wouldn't say the work was fun or fulfilling. Once settled at camp, in the jungle, I ran a remote radio relay station. The only bright spot was that, in this midst of all of this, I met a girl.

It's a known fact that mental illness is higher among soldiers and military members. Many return home racked by PTSD and anxiety, caused by combat, separation from loved ones, and the dehumanizing nature of the military. Veterans all over the country are out of work, traumatized and without aid for the debilitating stress they experienced as a result of serving their country. This is not to bash the military, or say that military service doesn't ever make a person a better version of themselves. Only that what goes in (especially if it's an undiagnosed mental illness) is likely to be amplified coming out. With the dramatic incline in veteran violence and suicide, the military is finally

being pressured to provide
reasonable mental health
treatment.

She had been a soldier for several years and
outranked me. It all started with some snide
comments about me being a newbie. I took the
bait, was hooked, and before too long she reeled
me in. First and foremost, she was a nurturer. She
mothered everyone; young or old, mentally ill or
sane, it didn't matter. She was the soldier who
drove the jeep mentioned earlier and served as the
mechanic for our team while we were deployed.
She was a gritty, fiery gal, from a small town in
Ohio and she was ten-years my senior. The best
thing about her was that she accepted me for who I
was - odd behavior and all. We were good partners
on the job and off the job. We weren't necessarily

in love, but we truly enjoyed each other's company.

Chapter 10

Finding the Light in all the Wrong Places

Two months had passed since my knee injury. It finally became so painful that I sought medical help. The Army doesn't move fast on medical issues, so they limited my physical activity, and a year later, in July of 1985, cleared me for surgery to clean out the floating shards of bone. They also dropped a life-changing bomb. News I had dreaded since the day of the accident. After the surgery, I'd be given an honorable medical discharge and sent home.

The reality of my situation hit me like a Mack truck. My life as I knew it was over. Everything I'd worked so hard for gone in an instant. There was no hope. At least that's what I told myself.

Utterly defeated, with no reason to live, I looked for peace at the bottom of a whiskey bottle. When I didn't find what I was looking for in the first bottle, I guzzled another. And another. And another.

I saw the white light. There was no sound, just total peace. I watched as the scene played out below. My brothers carried my body back to our room, lifted it onto a bunk, and called for help. The ambulance showed up and began CPR. They did their job well. Too well. I was back.

The peaceful white light was gone. All I could see now was panicked faces, tubes, wires and the artificial box light on the ceiling of the ambulance. They strapped me to a gurney since my size and intoxication made me difficult to manage.

What they didn't know (but were about to find out) was that being confined is a little slice of hell for me. On top of that, I was really pissed to be back.

The memory is like a flip book. Scenes of desperation, sorrow, anger and honest-to-God fury. With the emotions building upon themselves exponentially, I ripped through the straps of the gurney, and unleashed a torrent of rage that caused more than $400 damage to the ambulance. You see, at that moment, the rescuer's help hadn't felt like a blessing. They had ruined my escape. We're told not to bite the hand that feeds us, but what about the hand that brings us back to life? If there's a rule on that, I didn't get the memo.

Eventually we arrived at the hospital, where I was heavily restrained with cuffs, bands and straps, so they could administer bag after bag of IV fluid which had me sobered up in less than two hours. Not long after, a Master Sergeant paid a visit to formally address my behavior. Surely, I would be punished, but I had already lost my place in the military and, as I saw it, didn't have much else to lose. When he got close to the bed, I suddenly lashed out again and, in a fit of blind rage, nearly snapped his arm with my restraint. He managed to pull free and escape a potentially devastating injury. When things settled down, and I got my wits about me, I profusely apologized for what I had done. He brushed it off and forgave me without thought. He was an older, wiser man, who understood and truly lived the value of the brotherhood. He spoke to me with emotional clarity and grace. In fact, he vouched for me to get a break, and furthermore, made me realize nothing good would come from the direction my life was headed. He didn't come right out and discuss my suicide attempt, but I knew that *he* knew what had really happened. I wasn't just a belligerently drunk young man. I was seriously unwell.

What happened later, or more importantly what *didn't* happen, is noteworthy. When I was pulled in and formally questioned about the incident, I simply replied 'I'm stupid.' They ordered me to an Alcoholics Anonymous (AA) meeting and called it good. Here I had put myself, medical personal, and even my own brother in harm's way yet was not given a psychological evaluation or counseling (let alone a diagnosis or medication). It all tied up very neatly from their perspective. I didn't die and they were discharging me a couple of months.

I barely participated at their AA meeting, since I didn't necessarily have an alcohol problem. At least I didn't think so at the time. It was my brain. It was completely obvious to me that something wasn't right in my head. Only alcohol could drown out the voice that screamed inside my head. But I wasn't about to say that out loud.

Chapter 11

The bullets land somewhere

Before leaving Panama, I had surgery on my knee. They removed the broken bits and I stayed in the hospital for more than five weeks to start the healing process. I had round-the-clock care and regular therapy. Perhaps it was the best place for me since I couldn't leave. Not one to let that stop my deviant behavior I had my friends sneak me liquor. Not long after getting out of the hospital, I was sent to Memphis, Tennessee, processed out, and honorably discharged (which we *all* know wouldn't have happened if they'd known what was at the bottom of that fourth bottle).

Next I purchased a Jeep and, with nowhere else to go, headed for my parents' home in Indiana.

When I rolled up and knocked, my oldest sister, who lived nearby, answered their door. Puzzled, I ask where mom and dad were, only to discover they had recently moved. Not across town but across the country to Utah. My sister was house sitting until the place sold. I wondered why they hadn't bothered to mention this 'minor' detail, and laughed to myself that maybe they didn't want to be found.

So, me being me, I went looking for them. They'd moved to Salt Lake City, which was a solid 24-hour drive. I set out to drive straight through, but the freeway was closed in Wyoming because of a blizzard. I got a hotel and decided to phone and tell them I was on my way. But when I called their house, my Grandma answered and told me they were out of town. The following day I continued to

Salt Lake City, found the house, and had a nice reunion with Grandma. Two days later my parents returned from their trip. Surprise! Guess who's home?

Now what? With my life turned upside down, I needed to figure out what to do. Getting a job seemed to be the first logical step so I applied and landed a glamorous position as a cashier at Kmart. Yep, I went from saving the world, with my brawn and bravery, to manning a check stand and stocking shelves. Adapting to civilian life was harder than I'd anticipated. Of course, I wasn't perfect in terms of fitting in, even *before* my service, but the military changes you. It wipes your slate clean and molds you into someone new. I didn't fit in to this 'outside' civilian world. Even light conversation felt unnatural. Not like the comfortably crude banter I had shared with my brothers. Instead, talking to people felt forced, and fake, and tedious. But what I hated most was dealing with the public.

I lasted a week. I just couldn't take it. Clearly there had to be more. I love to ski, so it made sense to look for a job at a ski resort. I found work almost immediately, manning a switchboard at Snowbird. The job was, at least, closer to what I had trained to do in the army. And during those months I made some new friends, including a girl I worked with. Right out of the gate she and I 'clicked.' Confined to the small switchboard room for 8 hours at a time, we talked a lot and joked around. After work, we drank beer at the resort bar. On our days off we skied. I was beginning to relax. After having my life altered so drastically this friendship was a beacon of hope.

But you know life. At least my life thus far. So, tighten your seatbelt, because here comes another curve. Two months later, in December of 1985, my phone rang. It turned out to be my girlfriend-in-arms, the nurturer, and come to find out, she was carrying my child.

Chapter 11

Unprepared, Unqualified, Unfit, Unnerved

"Should I keep it?" she asked me.

When you hear these stories there's usually a
reaction of emotion like excitement, or anger, or
shock. Mine was different. For me, everything
stopped, and there was a brutal, deafening silence -
inside my head, on the phone line, and in the room
where I stood. Silence. The ultimate nothing. I
had no idea what to say, let alone what to do. I
hadn't ever really given significant thought to it; I
mean, me having a kid? I wasn't even much good
at *being* a kid, let alone raising or being responsible
for one. My life decisions thus far hadn't been
directed by much of anything other than selfish
desire or my passion for the military. Maybe this

was an opportunity to do something right. Maybe having a child would be a way of choosing a new life path, and provide the motivation to make good decisions. I was only 19, and I wasn't ready, but is anyone ever really "ready?"

No one would argue that I was unfit, for a long list of reasons, to be a father. But the thought of abortion went against my gut. Now was the time for action. Though we weren't in love, I thought we could make it work. I knew she would be a great mother. Maybe, with her by my side, I could be a great father too.

We agreed to keep our baby together. It felt odd; I would never in my life have predicted this was going to happen. Two months later, in February of 1986, she came to Salt Lake City,

accompanied by my old military bunkmate. The
reunion brought inspiration and hope. Perhaps the
past following me wasn't such a bad thing.
Besides, I had not really set roots in Salt Lake City.
My new purpose was the child my girlfriend was
carrying.

She had "orders" to report to Ft. Belvoir in
Virginia, in four weeks, for Non-Commissioned
Officer (NCO) training. So, we packed up the jeep
and began a whirlwind trip across the country so I
could meet her family. As we traveled, I realized
this wasn't new to her. You see, she already had
five marriages behind her (I know, I know!).
Anyway, her family were great people, but it was
obvious that their expectations for our success
weren't necessarily set very high.

We went from Arizona to Ohio, and finally landed in Virginia, where she reported for duty. The day she showed up, and they realized she was pregnant, she was told she could not attend school. Fortunately, the Army had use for her elsewhere, and, with uncharacteristically lightning speed, they re-assigned her to Ft. Bliss, Texas, to manage their motor pool. We turned around and headed directly for El Paso.

El Paso is nice, especially for a city in the middle of the desert, but the job market was suffering brutally. Gangs and drugs were rampant. Finding work was hard enough. Moving up was nearly impossible. I landed a job at Denny's, bartending and waiting tables, and began saving as much money as I could. After our first trip to the grocery store, I quickly realized the job wouldn't be enough to provide for my family. I had to find something else. I ground through a few more months at the restaurant before finding a full-time job bartending. It was a scene I was used to, but this time I was on the other side of the bar (and the other side of bar brawls too).

On June 16th, 1986 I became a father to a healthy baby boy. I was in the room when he was born, and though I was happy he had finally arrived, I was also but truly conflicted. Joy quickly turned to horrible desperation. What if turns out like me? Oh God - what have I done? Slipping into despair, I left the hospital, broke down, and cried. Not knowing what to do next, I did the only thing I could think of. I went to the bar.

We discussed marriage but my girlfriend resisted. No surprises there. I felt it was important, though, and persisted. Finally, she gave in, and in August, when our baby was two months old, we had a small ceremony before the Justice of the Peace in El Paso. We got a keg of beer and threw a party afterward to celebrate. I wasn't gloriously happy, but I thought I was doing the right thing by her and my son.

About nine months after the baby was born, my wife was transferred to Ft. Carson, in Colorado Springs, so we picked up and headed for the mountains. I found part time work at two different restaurants, at the opposite ends of town, and a third job framing homes, which left very little time to bond with my young son. The pressure to perform and provide was unparalleled. I was doing what I could to keep everything together but my date with disaster was imminent.

Within a year our marriage was beginning to unravel. In spite of the fact that I worked three jobs, it seemed we were always broke. I was frustrated with my wife's irresponsibility with our limited resources. When we didn't have cash, she'd write a bad check for something as small as a pack of cigarettes. After a few $30 overdraft charges, for a $1.99 item, I got fed up and insisted we keep separate accounts. We bickered with more regularity. Eventually I told her I wanted out; it just wasn't working.

"No, no, you need me," she'd plead.

This raised my ire even more.

"No, I *don't* f-ing *need* you!" I'd answer, angry at her presumption.

Inside, I felt more and more nuts as the days went by, and was becoming consumed with self-defeating talk.

Chapter 12
No Control, No Alternative, Delete
(CTRL+ALT+DELETE)

I knew the more I invested into this family, the more they were invested in me. My thorough disappointment in myself was killing me inside, and it was only a matter of time before it crept out and finished me off. Maybe that was the answer. Maybe it would be better if my son didn't remember his crazy father. I wanted to make an exit, but I had to do it the right way. At least, the right way in my mind. The crazy way.

The plot was born when I met a woman who was more 'bat shit crazy' than I was. She the perfect complement to *my* crazy. Even better, she would serve as the perfect excuse to exit both my marriage and my life. To make that happen, I brought her home one night, took her into the bedroom next to where my wife and son were sleeping, and had sex with her. The next morning, the woman and I exited the bedroom, sat down in the kitchen, and I announced to my wife

"There will be three for coffee."

Yes, I was a real asshole. I purposefully, blatantly, threw my affair in my wife's face in order to get out of the marriage. Looking back, I know it was hateful and disrespectful, but to my distorted mind, it was my only method of escape. I saw it as an insurance policy that ensured she would let me go and never take me back. I didn't want her to be able to forgive me, so I made the decision, and made certain I was stuck with it.

Everything went as planned. My wife picked up the baby, packed a few things, and left. Strangely, she didn't even seem mad. I opened a bottle of whiskey and started the familiar practice of escape. Before long, I found myself sitting in a chair in the living room, with a loaded .45 caliber pistol in my hand. I could smell the metal as my hand sweated around the grip - I can still smell it. The smell of cessation. The smell of pure relinquishment of worldly responsibility.

Satan was there that day too, in physical form, as clear as day. Smiling. Watching. Waiting for me to end it. That made me REALLY angry, and I took my finger off the trigger. Out loud, through streaming tears, I screamed,

"You can't have me! I'm already taken!"

Even though I was ready to take my life, I knew that God loved me, understood my complete desperation, and would welcome me back to the light. I just had to declare it out loud.

Next, I called my mother and father to let them know I loved them, and that things weren't working for me. The fear that had secretly haunted my father (that I'd die before reaching age 30), was finally come to fruition. There I was, 22 years old, ready to say goodbye upon my own accord. But I didn't give myself enough time. As I was taking the last swig of liquor there was a furious knock at the front door.

"Police, open up!"

I froze. This wasn't part of my plan. I couldn't even fathom how law enforcement had arrived so quickly, but, in hindsight, I am certainly glad they did. I later found out that my father had contacted police and, because he was also law enforcement, my rescue was likely expedited. It wasn't *just* the local police. An ambulance, the fire department, and the sheriff also showed up. A regular party and me the guest of honor!

The Sheriff talked to me. Looking back, he was a kind and gentle man. He was calm and cool. He wasn't concerned about the gun - he only wanted me to be safe. To me, though, it was only another soiled plan, where my decisions were either undermined or made by someone else. Not only did they take away my choice to die, they booked me into jail, on a 72-hour hold. First though, they took me to the hospital. The staff there were unbelievably kind in spite of the fact that I had bloody cuts all over my arms (yes, self-inflicted) and was clearly insane. The kindness ended when I was taken to jail; there was little interaction and they wanted nothing to do with me. To them, I was crazy, and they were just parking me for a few days. I find it kind of funny that society didn't want ME to take care of my problem (granted, death is an extreme way to do that), but *they* didn't want to deal with it either.

I'd been arrested wearing only my blue jeans. After three days, they let me out of jail wearing those same jeans. No shoes, no shirt, no wallet - nothing. It was about 50 degrees outside (there was still snow on the ground) and I had to walk until I found a phone. Hey, thanks Colorado Springs! As I left, they told me I was expected to appear in court in a few days, or they'd issue a warrant for my arrest.

Being tried for attempting suicide is a disgusting concept and one that I am not willing to accept. If someone is in such crisis that they're willing to put a gun to their head, a rope around their neck, or swallow a bottle of pills, there should be treatment. Yes, the 72-hour hold kept me from harming myself further, but ultimately, it was another huge missed opportunity for intervention. People in this position desperately want some answers! They're alone, scared, and feel like they're out of options. Sometimes, just a little human kindness and interaction can go a long way.

Chapter 13
A turn in the Grinder

I wasn't sticking around to find out what they were going to do to me. I took off for my sister's place in Georgia. I drove for two days and arrived with just one dollar in my pocket. We are talking dead broke. Literally. A dead man walking with nothing to his name. Clearly, I was going to have to find a job, and quickly. But first, I went to my sister's house. She and her husband welcomed me, but I wouldn't say they were exactly glad to see me.

I landed a position at a food processing plant, making pre-formed seafood and onion rings. My job was to get into a bin of ground shrimp, and make sure they came out in a perfectly formed, marketable shape on the other side. Only God knows what actually went into the machine, let alone what came out. In spite of a deep division between races, I clicked with the black women at the plant. They were some of the most wonderful and hilarious people I'd ever met in my life, and they didn't judge me because I was white, crazy, sometimes, stupid. We were one. I was only able to enjoy their company for about a month before I couldn't take the work anymore, but I'll remember them always (and they were absolutely worth being banned from the white lunch table).

After the processing plant, I began bartending and bouncing for a nightclub. It was familiar territory and I enjoyed it. I met a lot of women, and there seemed to be no limit to how much sex I could have. But even with this risky behavior, I managed to continue to dodge the bullets.

The crazy girl (the one I slept with to destroy my marriage) flew in from Colorado to be with me. My sister, who had a young family, didn't condone my lifestyle and flat-out said "you can't stay here." I didn't blame her, and I couldn't argue. We found sanctuary in a hotel with a bed like a soup bowl and cockroaches roaming the walls and floors. Now, I nearly forgot to mention the smell, or maybe I repressed it. I'll leave it to your imagination.

I wasn't okay living in these conditions and insisted that the crazy girl get a job to aid in our stability. Being off the rails, like me, and having a highly volatile temper, she fought the idea, and our relationship became even more toxic. Eventually she relented and got a job at the local Piggly Wiggly. That didn't last long.

To make matters worse, the drama and stress in the bar was enough to kill a horse. One particular night, things really hit a high note. My manager asked me to remove a loud, belligerent guest. If we're all being honest, I was happy to do it. I even enjoyed it, which speaks to how twisted I was upstairs. Later it came back to haunt me. The belligerent man, it turned out, was a local drug lord, and he placed a 'hit' on me. Luckily, I was warned to get out of town. Quickly. I couldn't take the chance that they'd hurt my sister or her family, so even in my manic mind, I didn't entertain the idea of staying.

I headed for my parents' house in Utah. The crazy girl tagged along as I headed West, but I was beyond sick of her, and I knew I couldn't take her to Salt Lake. We were like poison to each other. Like salt to plants. Death. So, I cut my losses and dropped her off in Colorado Springs with nothing but a blanket and her bag. What's worse is I didn't even feel bad. Actually, I didn't have even a *morsel* of remorse.

"You're on your own," I said as I left her at the curb. But the more I think about it, the more I see that statement was directed at myself.

So, I kept west until I landed in Salt Lake City, and picked up exactly where I had left off a few years back. I got a job at Snowbird running a snow cat in the winter, and working construction over the summer. Things were beginning to settle down and feel normal. And for a brief time, they actually were.

Chapter 14

The Kaleidoscope of Love

My second wife could be described as a true Southern belle. From the time I first met her, I knew she was different; she provided a feeling I craved but never realized I was missing. Everything about her invited me in. There were no judgements, and I could see myself being balanced out by her calm and loving demeanor.

I met her in Salt Lake City at the Cotton Bottom Inn, a little beer joint on the south end of town, famous for their delicious garlic burger (rightfully so). There, amidst the dark decor, the sound of the pool balls being racked, loud 70's rock and roll, and the n stench of garlic mixed with stale beer, I spotted a pretty girl, walked up, and asked for her number.

We went back there again for our first few dates. I'm lucky I didn't lose her straight off, because on our second date, I acted like an idiot and nearly started a brawl. Some young drunk guys sitting next to us were splashing beer on us as they made trips back and forth to the bar. It was innocent enough, but it was getting annoying, and when they spilled an entire beer down my back, I officially lost it. I'm the first to admit that, while it was a pretty disrespectful and infuriating thing for them to do, my reaction was way over the top. I stood up, turned around, grabbed their pitcher of beer, and hurled the contents all over them. I demanded an apology. When they refused, I invited them outside so I could kick their asses. In my mind (and in my rage), I could take on five to eight men. I was defending our honor.

I stormed outside, ready to take on the whole group, but my bravado quickly deflated, because no one followed. Inside, unbeknownst to me, a friend of mine was explaining the seriousness of this situation to the young men, and encouraging them to do the wise thing. Ultimately, they bought me a beer and apologized, we shook hands, and all was forgotten. Phew - crisis averted - and in spite of my asinine macho behavior, sweet belle continued to see me. I was thrilled because instinctively I knew I needed someone like her in my life to keep things stable.

She had great roots. Her parents were salt of the earth and our families immediately hit it off.

Surrounded by this support, our relationship flourished. Everything didn't just seem great, it *was* great. Things were so good we moved in together. She had two wonderful kids; a daughter and a son. As a father who was now separated from *his* son, I honestly wanted to be a constructive pillar in their lives. Unfortunately, I failed in more ways than one.

My new girlfriend worked as a Registered Nurse and had a good job. But she suffered from constant back and neck pain from injuries sustained in a car rollover a year earlier. Me being a 'fix-it' guy, I tried my best to bring her comfort and make life easier for her, and she tried to help fix my (very obvious) problems and help me get my life together. My money situation was dire. I had spent all I had on frivolous things during a manic episode, I had bad credit, and the repo men were after my car. Then there were my other bad 'habits' like fighting, drinking and risk-taking. But she loved me anyway. And I truly loved her.

I worked as a carpenter and a banned substance sales representative who specialized in cocaine. Strapped, and desperate for cash, I even signed up as a subject for medical experiments at our local university. While it wasn't glamorous, it *was* MUCH more legal than one of my other modes of revenue. Eventually, I worked my way out of my financial pothole and we bought a house in a working-class neighborhood outside of Salt Lake City. For a while I caught myself thinking I was getting better because we had a nice house, and were moving up in the world. But that's all it was. A nice house. My mental health had not improved.

A few months after moving in, we got married in the living room of our new house, surrounded by family and close friends. It was 1992. I vividly remember her insisting on a 'real' red velvet cake for the celebration made with beets and chocolate (for the red color, you know, old school). It was delicious, but the next day, we received a frantic phone call from a guest.

"My kids are pooping red! What did you feed my children? They're pooping red!"

Laughing, I told her it was just the cake, and that they'd be fine (beets in equals red out). I still laugh about it today. I mean, it's *me*. They should have expected something weird would happen at my wedding.

With our newfound stability we started attending church. The Baptist church to be exact. I had always believed in God. Maybe the answers to my problems were as simple as giving it over, as the preacher said, and that my sinful ways were blocking my redemption. So, I agreed to be baptized.

I think I expected to feel differently right away but that's not what happened. Not only did I NOT feel better, I felt even worse. I can't even get *this* right. So, I tried again. And again, five times in all over that five-year period, thinking *one* of these times it had to take! But the church and their rituals weren't enough to overcome the unwanted demon inside me.

My new wife introduced me to a lot of great people - nurses, doctors and the like, which undoubtedly made my life better. I still had a hard time building long-term friendships, but these people were good to me, and were there for me when I needed them. One was even kind enough to remove a bone tumor from my arm. They also bailed me out a handful of times when I was taking unnecessary risks at work, but was too macho to report injuries to my employer. Once, I slipped off a huge snow cat and ruptured two discs in my back. Another time we were cutting saplings on the mountain with chainsaws. I grabbed the only chainsaw without a chain brake, because, of course, I didn't want anyone to get hurt. Did I foreshadow enough here? I nearly took my hand off at the wrist then tried to hide the accident. Thank God for out doctor friends who patched me up. If I could give advice to anyone, it's that it takes more courage to say something than not to. It's clear now (with education, experience, and hindsight) how important it is to take care of yourself both physically and mentally, because they go hand in hand. Unless you cut one off with a chainsaw.

Chapter 15
When Your Poker Face Malfunctions

Before too long I had a manic episode. This one had me convinced there was nothing but doom remaining for us in Salt Lake City, so I called for a move to the Dallas area. Dallas was booming and I told myself that was where I was going to make my fortune. We moved, and right away my wife found her dream home, on an acre of land, in a small town outside Dallas. Despite having money from the sale of our home in Salt Lake, we couldn't purchase the property until I had a job. So, I applied and quickly landed a job as a foreman with a company in Plano, Texas, building a bridge. This was the start to an extraordinary time in my life, and not necessarily in a good way.

Shortly after starting the job in Plano, I made a really good friend at work. This was unusual, but welcome, because I'd had such a hard time establishing lasting friendships. He was a great guy and a good confidant. One day, while my friend and I were eating lunch at a restaurant, my head started to feel really strange. Then I noticed my friend staring at me. He looked extremely concerned. Finally, he spit it out,

"I think you're having a stroke!" he said, nervously.

It's hard keeping friends when you're bipolar. Often, they get the wrath of the aggressive, hypomanic mind, and after that, they don't stick around to find out the reason. What's worse? We *know* what we did and said to our friend - a person who didn't deserve bad treatment. And unlike a drunk who blacks out and has no memory of their bad behavior, *we* have to live with the memory of being hostile or rude. We know *exactly* what we did. The shame and remorse are a heavy burden on our hearts. After a while we just quit apologizing because we're too embarrassed and discouraged. We realize we've driven away yet another friend. Eventually it just doesn't matter anymore.

By now the entire right side of my face had started to droop and I had no muscle control. I don't like ambulances. You may have remembered. So instead of calling for help, or letting my friend help me, I drove *myself* to the hospital. That was stupid, I know, but that's what I did. When I arrived, my blood pressure was a whopping 270/220. Excitedly, the nurse said,

"Sir, you need to calm down."

Thanks lady. That's helpful.

The hospital staff quickly determined that this was not a stroke but Bell's Palsy, a condition that can be brought on by extreme stress. The expectations of my demanding job, coupled with the stress of just being me - living in my crazy head every day and just trying to act normal - were finally taking their toll as a physical manifestation. Fantastic! Cause I didn't already have enough problems.

In the following five or six years, I went through many jobs. My wife was doing well in her occupation and was climbing the ladder, however, her back and neck pain were getting worse, and her health was declining. My mental health was suffering too. The highs and lows were becoming more regular for me.

It's not uncommon for people with bipolar disorder to job hop or get fired a lot.

The bipolar person sees much, within their job, that can be criticized; management is stupid, things are poorly done, and the bipolar person is easily triggered. They're typically quite literal, and if management tells them something, they expect the *exact* thing they were told.

By contrast, to management the bipolar person appears to be a loose cannon. They're not quiet about their opinions, and can be perceived as scary, over aggressive, or unapproachable.

Bottom line, if you're bipolar, the littlest thing can trigger you to quit your job (before they fire you).

During this time, I had an amazing, life changing experience. My wife and I were attending a local Baptist church, where we became friendly with a lady who had just been diagnosed with terminal brain cancer. She had a young family - a husband and three children under twelve. For some reason (still unbeknownst to me), she stopped me after the service one Sunday and asked me for my guidance, telling me she'd been on the hunt for 'the right church.' She was hoping that she'd find this "right" place before she passed.

My heart broke for her.

"You're looking for the wrong thing," I said.

"Look for *your* God, and by *your* God, I mean, not a building, a place, a community, or a religion. You show *your* God how *you* believe, because <u>*your faith is carried with you*</u>," I finished.

Nearly a year later, as her disease had progressed and she was nearing the end, I had another intimate discussion with her. By then, my wife and I had become close with her and her husband. We'd been to their house, with other members of our church, doing service projects and trying to make their life, and transition, a little easier. I was amazed, and humbled, and honored, when she told me.

"I found God, thanks to you."

Me? Seriously? Advice from me? What an honor. That *had* to be divine intervention.

She died not long afterward. We stayed close with her husband and tried to support their young family after her passing. Why had God used me as His conduit? I don't know and I don't care. I'm just glad He did.

As my periods of mania and happiness faded, my depression and self-loathing became so dark, deep, and extreme that I turned, once again, to that bottle of caramelly Jack Daniels. Good 'ol Jack. He was my doctor for the longest time. My wife caught on to what I was doing and wasn't happy that I would come home angry after drinks. I'd stumble in the door and (regrettably) butt heads with her son who began to abhor me. I don't blame him, but at the time I saw his reactions to me as personal and unjustified. Here I had wanted to be a hero to this family. Now I was nothing but a villain. Entangled in apathy, my behavior was more than toxic, it was dangerous.

The manic episodes were fleeting and the distance between my wife and me was growing. When my wife would go out of town, I'd spend thousands of dollars at strip clubs and casinos, or dining in lavish nature, to appease my narrowing windows of mania. The withdrawal stage of my relationship, as I'd experienced before, had begun.

Having an untreated Bipolar Disorder inside a relationship is like an ocean without the moon to control the tide. Emotions ebb and flow, turning quickly from a glassy surface into a Tsunami. This is hard enough for the person suffering from mental illness, but that person's partner and family members also have the difficult task of navigating those turbulent waters. The pressure of living with this feeling is enough - it's no wonder relationships don't withstand the stress.

Chapter 16
Wet paper bag

I knew I needed help. Something was *very* wrong with me and it continued to destroy everything good. Desperate for things to be different, I made a very difficult phone call to my sister (the doctor), admitted I was in trouble, and asked for her help. I knew I could count on her. She was someone I could trust and whose opinion of me wouldn't falter even if she knew I had something amiss in my head. Her first recommendation was to have an evaluation by a psychiatrist. Since she lived in a different state, she did some research and called me back with a name. Of course, she couldn't have known what was to come, but the doctor I rolled up on put the A in Apathy. After seeing him, and spilling my guts about what I thought was going on, he told me I was an alcoholic, gave me samples of Depakote (a medication for depression), and told me to call in two weeks if I didn't feel better. He honestly couldn't have cared less if I died in my bed last night. I left, completely dejected. I KNEW there was something more wrong with me and this guy hadn't even *tried* to hear me or listen. And the alcohol? Yes, I drank all the time, and way too much, but only so I could cope. Why couldn't anyone see that this was a symptom not a cause? I left his office, threw the pills in the trash, and bought a bottle of Jack.

It's SO unfortunate that I wasn't taken seriously by this clown. I wonder now if I'd had a proper diagnosis and correct medication

150

at this juncture in my life if I could have saved my second marriage and my family. And I wonder, too, how many other people, like myself, finally find the courage to reach out for professional help only to be dismissed by some pompous, judgmental, jerk. Fortunately, I only grabbed a bottle of booze on the way home. How many grab a gun?

Throughout the end months of my marriage to my second wife, I would chug a fifth (if not more) of whiskey on the drive home from whatever job I had landed at the time. It was the only thing I could do to cope with what was going on in my head. She could smell it on me, see it in my eyes, and had to experience the worst parts of me. When she did confront me, I had extremely erratic behavior. Once, when an argument exploded in the kitchen, I'm told I pissed in the refrigerator as an act of aggression. I'd had so much to drink I don't remember the incident. We are talking pure blackout of mind, body, and empathy for those around me. In a similar instance, and one of our final arguments, I was cooking myself some macaroni and cheese. When my wife saw how drunk I was, and asked me to leave, I angrily picked up the hot pan and slammed it, as hard as I could, in the sink.

Our most hurtful behaviors are often reserved for those who love and care for us most deeply. After hiding all day outside of our safe zone, from an unforgiving society who doesn't understand or accept mental illness, we get home and unleash all the pent-up anger, anxiety and frustrations upon our undeserving spouse or family.

By now, I had clearly lost all regard for the wellbeing of my wife, her kids, and myself. She finally drew the line. She would no longer allow my behavior to affect the lives of her children. At the end, there were no fights. We existed more as a roommate than husband and wife. She avoided me to protect herself. We slept in separate beds, avoided eye contact and conversation, and would walk past each other as if we didn't even know each other.

In hindsight, it wasn't reasonable to expect my wife to navigate the troubled waters of my mental illness within our relationship, but I *do* think she knew there was something bigger than alcoholism at work here, though neither of us could identify or understand it.

With divorce papers in the works I moved out of that beautiful dream house and became instantly homeless. I don't remember the exact day, and don't pity me. At least not for that. I would stay in my truck or a hotel now and then, but my mind was more of a disaster than my housing situation. I was losing my shit. I worried that others could see my mental illness and that if anyone found out I'd lose my job.

Finally, on Pearl Harbor day, December 7th, our divorce was final. All this symbolism! Thinking back on the day, I have to say that this was one of the worst times of my life. I was drunk all day, every day, and I believe the alcohol robbed me of most of those memories. It can keep them.

I really truly loved my wife and the kids, but it's clear that we had to separate for their sake. What I did to them was horrible. Talking about it now, bringing these feelings to the surface, cuts like a knife. Losing people is one of the hardest parts of mental illness because people make you feel better. My second wife taught me that. I'm forever indebted to her and feel blessed that she has forgiven me. Those who have shown me this grace are few and far between.

Chapter 16

When there's Nothing, there's Someone, and that's a Problem

By this point I had given in to my illness in its entirety. I was in pure survival mode and that created the "perfect storm" and catalyst for me to slide right into my next mistake, a super dysfunctional relationship with a woman from work.

I met her on a job at Dallas Airport in August of 2001, a few months before my divorce was final. She knew I was living in my truck and offered me a place to stay and sex, which was a problem in the big scheme of things, considering who was in a failing marriage with two kids. Yet there was something about her. She made me feel like a man and fed my delusions of grandeur. I drained my bank account wining and dining her. When I was with her, the negativity didn't permeate my life. Probably because, by comparison, she had so much shit of her own.

At some point, she invited me home to stay with her overnight. By now she had filed for divorce from her husband "because he wasn't putting out," and though he still lived with her in the home, she kicked him out for the night. I was a prime candidate to fill his position. She was a sexual banshee, with an insatiable appetite, and we'd go all night. It bears noting that I was told to be gone before her two girls woke up for school. I think they probably figured it out anyway. Or, they were used to it. Who knows? I was in the 'don't

care about the sack of puppies on the highway'
mindset at this point.

We continued this way until I finally landed
an apartment right outside the South entrance of the
airport. This gave us nearly unlimited meeting
opportunities for our "extracurricular activities."
We met up in the early morning, at lunchtime, after
work, and in the evening. I didn't actually realize
the depth of her sexual addiction until years later,
but she had all sorts of unusual behaviors, like
keeping a tally of every sexual encounter.
According to her records, we hooked up exactly
385 times that first year. Maybe it's hard to
fathom, but that's a lot. Too much. I don't care
who you are; it was exhausting. And I didn't even
get a participation award.

Not surprisingly, she'd experienced a rough childhood. She was given up for adoption at an early age and later went into foster care, which had been volatile and sometimes abusive. Eventually she was adopted, but as a young teenager started drinking and running away. By 15 she was pregnant, didn't know who the father was, and her parents kicked her out of the house. She made her way to Las Vegas, only to have another child with a drug addict there. Just more bad luck with bad decision icing. Unfortunately, I understood. I made terrible decisions all the time too. But maybe we were drawn to each other because of our mutual dysfunction. Like I said, she was a catalyst in my decline but, then again, I didn't say "No."

She had a string of corrupted marriages in her wake. We got along mostly well considering neither of us had a solid grasp on healthy relationships or any stability in general. We spent money freely, hopping airplanes like it was a hobby, and taking impromptu surfing trips to California. It was a beneficial arrangement for that time of my life -- a long manic episode. On occasion she'd bring another woman home for a threesome. It was a crazy man's dream. Later she'd be mad that I'd gone along with it (yes, in spite of the fact that it was *her* idea) because it played into her insecurities. But honestly, that was the least of our worries.

Chapter 17
Drink, Rinse, Repeat

One day, when my mania hit with intensity of a laser, frying all inhibition, I went to the airport, flew from Texas to Los Angeles, and rented a shiny red convertible. Celebration ensued all the way to Laguna Beach (drinking, eating, eating, drinking) where I parked the car and passed out on the cliffside. My girlfriend, still at home in Texas, sent a posse out looking for me, but luckily (or maybe un-luckily), I was hidden well. It was one day and night of pure surrender to my manic mind that had involved *so* much alcohol I couldn't remember it anyway. That is until I woke up to find my red fancy toy. The morning after was worse than being chewed up, spit out and shit on. There was no removing the taste or the smell of all that partying from my mouth. The best I could do was rinse with some Jack and start another booze bender.

Not having better sense, and not caring for my safety, I found my way to Compton, deciding I wanted Roscoe's chicken and waffles. What a delight! Seriously. The friendly staff gifted me a T-shirt for bravery, telling me this area wasn't meant for white folk. I recall similar events of luck and kindness, but I was now past the point of a downward slide. My behavior was going to kill me and I didn't care.

This is the dumpster alley of my life. It was intense, dramatic, and consumed by absolute chaos. My manic episodes were less and less fun, because there was always hell to pay afterward. Ultimately, they became just as devastating as the depressive episodes. About this time, an old friend from high school showed up on the scene. She'd come looking for me. She had so many mental health issues of her own, like anorexia, bulimia, and suicide attempts, that the State had just taken away her only child. She was out of options, looking to be saved, and I was the candidate. She convinced me she understood me and wanted to take care of me. I went away with her for a short time - leaving my girlfriend - but it didn't take long to realize that two sick people were not better as one. I sent her packing. My girlfriend was pissed but she took me back.

We decided to take a flight to Atlanta and see my nephew graduate high school using airline miles. With my delusions of grandeur in full swing, we partied like rock stars. On the way back to Texas, we were involuntarily 'bumped' from our flights a couple times. We took it in stride and hopped the next plane, ultimately taking five separate legs in first class. Though the drinks in first-class are free, we treated this amenity like it was a booze spigot (fully open). The plane landed safely but I was crashing. Intoxicated and exhausted, we hopped a cab to get out of the airport.

Chapter 18

How Much is the Fare to Insanity?

What happens next isn't something I'm proud of. Upon exiting the cab, the driver requested the fare of thirteen dollars. Thirteen! What? My intoxicated self was not aware that the fare out of the airport was so high and I wasn't happy about it. Looking back, I had just flown first class, spent who-knows-how-much on gifts, food, and partying, and I was triggered by a cab fare? That stupid thirteen dollars nearly cost me 20 years in a penitentiary.

The cab driver and I had "words" about the transaction which led to a fight and, in short, I beat the guy up. Once my girlfriend realized I'd lost it, she insisted on driving my truck home. She jumped in the driver's seat and argued with me. When she wouldn't let me in, I shattered the window of my own truck! My truck.

> The emotions felt during a Bipolar shift are unmeasurable and even more unfathomable. It's emotional pain in the most concentrated form. Mine in this moment was rage.

I should have listened to her. But no. In the end, I left her there, and took off in my glass-laden truck, with an arm slashed open from the remainder of the window. Predictably, she called and reported the incident to the police.

I just wanted to get home. Just outside the airport I was stopped by the police. They weren't the brightest or the most competent. Surprisingly, they hadn't stopped me because of my girlfriend's call. They'd decided to pull me over since they'd 'sensed something was wrong.' That is about the only thing they were right about.

"Is there anything wrong here, sir?" They had asked.

"Nope," I slurred.

"You're bleeding, Sir."

"Ah, would you look at that. I had to break my window to get in," I explained.

"Have a great night!"

They left, but I wasn't off the hook. Not by a long shot. The next day I got a call from the Airport police. I was being charged with Aggravated Assault and Bodily Injury for beating up the cab driver. A first-degree Felony with a possible sentence of up to 20 years in prison. They suggested I find an attorney, told me my bond was fifty grand, and told me to turn myself in.

Now fifty-thousand dollars is a lot of money for someone who spends it as he earns it. What this meant for me was that I would have to rely on my girlfriend to get me at least five thousand dollars for bond. I didn't want to be beholden to her, because I knew she'd use it against me, but now she had me firmly by the cojones and we both knew it.

I lament what I lost of myself that day, but it's also what drove me to become the best I can be. Accepting my past and my mistakes was the first step.

Chapter 19
Hard Pills to Swallow

It's then that I realized I had transformed into something I wasn't, and someone I didn't want to be. It's not a feeling I'd wish on my worst enemy. So I took a drastic step that day that I believe saved my life. I got online and did some research. I had to get to the bottom of this. I realized that this thing I had *must* be some type of mental illness, and that there had to be some help out there. I got my courage up, picked up the phone, and made an appointment with a psychiatrist in Dallas.

Ultimately, it took the fear of prison to drive me to recovery and answers. Research has since become one of the key components to my success. An abundance of information is now at the fingertips of anyone with curiosity. Become educated so you can represent yourself. Educating yourself doesn't make you an expert, but *ask questions*. Provide alternatives you may have learned or simply request what you think you need. Be your own advocate.

The day of the appointment I made my girlfriend come with me. I knew if I didn't have someone there to keep me honest, I'd lie to the guy. I'd lied so much over the years, to cover up who I really was, it was second nature. He turned out to be a kind, wise, white haired, grandfatherly fellow, who had been practicing for many years. He took time with me and listened. He asked questions. And at the end of the appointment he told me I have Bipolar I Disorder, that he'd get me on medications right away, and that I'd be taking them the rest of my life. He also said some of the most healing, and freeing words anyone has ever said to me.

"When you walk out this door today, you'll leave behind all of the negative feelings, regret, and shame."

And I did. When I left, I felt different? The burden and shame of my past was miraculously lifted. And finally, a diagnosis! An answer! A name for this demon! FINALLY. I was 37 years old.

I implore you; if you see something, say something. It's a little maddening (yes, pun intended) to look back on how many opportunities there were, over 37 years, to intervene on my behalf, and no one did! I'm not angry about that, hindsight being 20/20 and all, but let's not let that happen to one more person. Clearly people knew something was off with me, and it's a miracle I made it as long as I did. Open your mouth, reach out your arms, give a shit, save a life.

Chapter 20

Strings Attached

A few months after my arrest, after living on pins and needles, I finally went to court and was sentenced. Besides the required restitution to the state of Texas (several thousand dollars), I received 4 years' probation with regular urine samples (to prove I wasn't drinking), alcohol and anger management classes, and 240 hours of community service. This was split between picking up trash along the side of the highway, community cleanups, patching potholes with asphalt, working in the library, and washing windows. The library was perhaps the most boring experience of my life (no offense to librarians and bookworms). But I attacked the hours with a vigor, worked hard, and completed in 11 months what they expected would

take two years. I'm Dave. I wasn't having it. I
needed it over with.

About half of all prison inmates
exhibit behaviors relative to
mental illness.

Just because sentencing was over, I wasn't
out of the woods. Probation meant I also had to
stay out of trouble. I straightened up, followed their
rules, and played by the book. Because one misstep, one false move, and I'd be sent straight to
prison. My girlfriend, as anticipated, used this to
her advantage. If we'd argue, about anything,
she'd trump me by saying,

"All I have to do is make one phone call, and tell your Probation Officer you're drinking, and you'll be sent straight to prison. Don't push me."

In hindsight, the ultimatum provided by my wife wasn't such a bad thing. Of course, at the time it left me feeling bitter and betrayed, but I have to wonder what would have happened if someone had put the hammer down sooner? Like my parents? Or the military? Or my first two wives? No, I wasn't happy about it, but I badly needed it.

It always had its intended effect. It shut me right up. And it also made me deeply resent her. I hated someone having that kind of control over me. I needed to gain some leverage. So, I asked her to marry me.

What? Yes, I know what you're thinking. How stupid can I be? But this tactical move also had its intended effect, and this time to *my* benefit. Now that she was giddily planning a wedding, the threats stopped. It bought me time. I needed just four years. We were married on a beach in California about 8 months later.

I started reading everything I could about my disease. Inside this new framework it made SO much sense! All those strange behaviors and feelings, way back to when I was a little kid, were actually pretty typical for someone with my disease. Excited, I bought books on Bipolar

Disorder for all my family members and sent them off in the mail. Not only did I expect it would help them understand me, I hoped it might also mend some fences, and lay the ground for some healing. After a few weeks I called around to discuss the book and all this fascinating new information with them. Not one had bothered to crack the cover.

While empathy is required to sustain a relationship with someone with a mental illness, let's touch on what's called 'empathy fatigue.' The understanding and willingness to stand by the side of a loved one, affected by mental illness, deteriorates over time and can turn, instead, to apathy. At a certain point your friend or loved one has 'been there and done that' with you, and they may not be as supportive as you'd have hoped.

If you're unable to interest your family and friends in your diagnosis, don't be surprised, and try not to be too quick to judge. You may have put them through a lot. To my sister's young family, for instance, I was now simply 'Crazy Uncle Dave.' The reasons, however compelling to me, no longer mattered to them.

Chapter 21
Medically induced Zombie

At that first meeting my psychiatrist had prescribed me three strong pharmaceuticals to manage my bi-polar, with the comment,

"You should see effects in a month or so. But, of course, everyone is different."

One week later they kicked in.

There are a couple of callous truths about medication and sunshine and rainbows isn't what I'm here to preach. First, there *is* no magic pill, and a pill doesn't take all the demons away. Medication isn't a cure. It's a tool in your toolbox of recovery.

Second (share this with your family and loved ones), prescribing the correct dose of medication is super tricky. It's like a driver's education teacher trying to overcorrect from the passenger seat -- of another car. My meds kicked in so quickly, and I went into such a deep, dark place so rapidly, that I wasn't even able to *identify* it as a problem to my doctor. I spent two years there.

Two. Years. Learn from my example. If you feel completely displaced, or your family notices you're blank, or in a fog, be in immediate contact with your doctor. Bipolar folks are often over-prescribed and end up in a dreary lithium 'coma.'

The change was dramatic. I was so heavily dosed that I flat-lined emotionally; sunk deep into a dark no-man's land. I was blank, restrained, impassive and entirely unreactive. Hey, I could win ten grand in the lotto! Nope, nothing. Children dying of starvation? Nope. No still nothing.

While accepting of the fact that I desperately needed to be on medication, I unknowingly signed away two years of my life to a medication-induced grey area. I expected smooth sailing, in a 'sunshine-on-the-wave's' kind of way. But reality came in a 'no-captain-at-the-helm-of-the-ship' kind of way.   It's like that period of my life was a big smear - written then erased with a crappy eraser.

THE 4 PILLARS OF RECOVERY

The mind a body are designed to work together. They're two pieces to one whole. If either is neglected, everything falls apart. If you can get your "Four Pillars of Recovery" in place, which include medication, support, exercise, and sleep, you'll be way ahead of the game.

Medication. Teamed with your doctor, seek a medication (or medications) that work for you. You might have a couple of false starts while you figure this out, but take accountability for your health; if your medication is not working, say so, and request a change. And, most importantly, once you *do* find medication that works for you, for heaven's sake, STAY ON IT! Taking your prescribed meds (in the correct doses and at the times you're told) needs to be part of your daily routine. It should be just as regular to your day as brushing your teeth.

Support/Therapy - find a therapist you mesh with. Just like medication, it may take a try or two before you find a therapist who "gets" you and whom you trust. Once you find this person stick with them; consistency is key to building this trust relationship. Make and keep regular appointments. Next, outside of your therapist, do you have people to call if you don't feel safe with yourself? Designate a few trusted people (ahead of time) that you'll call if that voice or other urges start getting out of control.

Exercise - get some form of exercise every day, ideally combined with some sunshine. A daily walk, outside, is ideal. To that end, eat regular meals. When you're depressed, eating can take a lot of energy and effort. It may be tempting to skip meals, but do what you can to get healthy food in daily. Have a back up plan for those days you don't feel like preparing food or eating.

Sleep - this one is tricky - especially if your medication isn't sorted out. When I was manic, and my mind was looking for stimulation, I'd stay up hours on end, partying and going to nightclubs, and getting maybe 3-4 hours of sleep per night. But this behavior couldn't go on forever and the crash was inevitable. I lost countless jobs because of this cycle.

The flip side can be just as vicious. When you're depressed, sleep can be your *only* lifeline (a means of escape for a few blissful hours), but ironically, the depression makes you dead tired all day, but unable to sleep at night.

Your doctor can prescribe medication for sleep at first. I found that once my other medications had me feeling more stable, sleep came naturally. I also found that keeping a schedule - going to bed at the same time and getting up at the same time - went a long way toward helping get back into a healthy pattern.

Eventually I had my medication dosage re-evaluated and ended up at a happy medium of medication vs. emotion. I was finally feeling <u>good</u> for the first time in my life. So good, I wanted to share this feeling with others. Out loud I said to myself,

"If I can just help just *ONE* person, maybe this will all have been worth it."

The opportunity came sooner than I thought. I happened to be working, for a couple of weeks, alongside a day laborer who seemed down on his luck. We got to talking and his story was heartbreaking. Just one-year prior he'd had a great job as a sports promoter, making $200, 000 per year, a nice home, and a wife and daughter, until things went completely sideways because of his untreated bipolar and he lost EVERYTHING. He even lost visitation rights to his daughter. He was now living in a bunk house, skinny as a rail, and going to the County for his treatment (though his medications and dosages were not yet dialed in). We talked at length. I told him about the four pillars of recovery and encouraged him to go back to the county, and not leave until they got him on the right medication, and the right dosage. I told him not to lose hope - he'd find his way out. Then my job changed and I lost track of him.

Eight months later, I was sitting on my favorite beach in California, my favorite place in the world, watching the waves crash on the beach, when my phone rang. It was the day laborer He'd called to thank me, tell me he'd gotten a job laying floor tile, had an apartment, and was seeing his daughter! I congratulated him and encouraged him to keep it going. After we hung up, I looked up toward the heavens and smiled. What a gift. There was my one person. It felt absolutely amazing. I wanted more of that feeling.

Considering its questionable start, my marriage actually wasn't all that bad. It wasn't all that good either but that can be said of many relationships. We got into house flipping for a while - she'd do the designs, and I'd oversee the work. My resentment for her still simmered beneath the surface though - I mean, how do you do that to someone you say you love? We made it a few more years before things got bad again. This time she accused me of an affair (no, I wasn't) and I'd had enough. I walked out on Christmas eve.

Like a boomerang returns to its source, I was making the same mistakes over (and over and over). But if I'm being really honest here, my three failed marriages can't be blamed on my ex-wife's behavior. *They* didn't choke out the relationships. I was the common toxic denominator.

Every relationship has its inevitable ebb and flow, but when bipolar disorder becomes part of the equation it's no longer only two people involved. Instead, it's you, your partner, and your bipolar self. The dynamic, which may have seemed simple at first, suddenly becomes extraordinarily complex.

We met up a few weeks afterward in a bar to discuss the end of our relationship, and she dropped a dozy on me - SHE was the one having the affair. That little tidbit sealed it for me. I knew I'd made the right decision, called a lawyer, and proceeded with a fast divorce. I was working a position that paid a stipend for living a certain distance from the job site. Now that I'd left my wife, and was living closer to the job, I was technically no longer entitled to the stipend. Feeling spiteful, my soon-to-be-ex threatened to tell my employer where I was living. Not one to be threatened, especially after living under the constant fear of her threats for so many years, I went out the very next day and purchased a house. A nice, BIG house. Nicer than hers. And wouldn't you know, it was just outside the boundary for my stipend? Did I mention I don't like to be threatened?

The divorce went smoothly, outside of the fact that she maxed out one of my credit cards after we separated, and took an exotic, expensive vacation with her children at my expense. That's okay. I got away. And I made an important decision the day the divorce was final, declaring out loud,

"I'm not going to hate her."

This proved to be one of the best things I ever did for myself. I stepped away from this chapter of my life not feeling any more anger, resentment, or *anything* really.

Chapter 22
The Oyster

As I began the next phase of my life, in a good place both mentally and emotionally, I decided to take the bull by the horns and discover more about myself, especially as it related to my disease. I was driven by the desire for a fix and for answers. What were the real and imagined powers of the monster in my head? Was there a monster at all? What is the meaning of the ups, and why do my downs go so low, below the floor, below sight of any who care? I wanted these 'pearls' of wisdom. So, I began the search for my 'oyster,' a therapist who could talk things through with me, unlock some of the answers and provide me some clarity.

Mental illness isn't something to be tackled alone. Accept it. We all believe we are strong enough to either just deal with it or fix it ourselves. Vocalizing and addressing your illness, as well as any discord which may have resulted from it, is vital. I, personally, had a difficult time adjusting to a regular schedule of anything, let alone dedicating time consistently to go in and talk with a therapist about my problems. But that's the wrong way to look at it. When you choose to commit

to treatment and attain a
scheduled regimen for
mental healthcare, you're
committing time to solutions,
not your problems. With the
right therapist it's a joint
effort to create the best life
for yourself. You don't
'deal' with it, you live with
it.

I found my first 'fit' with a Ph.D. of
Psychology, and started down my personal road to
understanding. It was amazing to truly connect
with a human being who understood, and had no
intention of judging me. Doors opened,
conversation flowed, and the 'fix' was provided,
from her mind to mine, through insightful ideas and

explanations. She was the first to really listen, and offer advice, and provide a haven from outside impulses. Our professional connection was so strong that after she moved to another state, I flew there once a month to continue my therapy. Losing momentum in my recovery and treatment was a living nightmare - one that threatened to swallow up my progress. Eventually, it had to come to an end (the cost was prohibitive) but I'm forever indebted to her for giving me a jumpstart I needed to really seek the best from myself.

Chapter 23
Utah Beckons

My phone rang one sunny winter day in 2012. It was my oldest sister. My dad, now in his early eighties, had collapsed and everyone was concerned. He was single handedly caring for our mother, whose Alzheimer's disease had progressed to the point that she was no longer able to care for herself. Each day he woke her, got her bathed and dressed, changed her bedding, did the laundry, cleaned the house, cooked her meals, fed her and gave her medications, did the dishes, did the laundry, took her for a walk, arranged and took her to doctor appointments, paid the bills, etc. etc. etc. He was suffering from exhaustion and some big changes needed to be made.

My sisters, for a variety of reasons, were not able to pick up and move to Utah. That left me. So, I quit my job, packed up my things, and left for the mountains. I helped where I could, and my dad got a much-needed break. His was an amazing display of love - he took care of her kindly, gently, and faithfully - just as he had promised in his marriage vows so many years earlier. And I got a much-needed break too. My career had become extremely demanding and had taken its toll on my health. I was overweight, hypertensive, and stressed out. In between helping with mom, I hired a trainer, started eating right, got myself hooked up at the local V.A. for medical care and psych treatment, and relaxed for the first time in a long time.

One individual is affected by Alzheimer's every sixty seconds. This staggering fact means each and every one of us is more than likely, if not certain, to encounter a loved one falling prey to his heartless predator. Imagine losing your short-term memory first, then the long term, then there's nothing left. Here's the kicker - the entire time you know exactly what's happening to you. At least until the end and there's nothing you or your family or healthcare professionals can do about it.

Six months after my return, I ran into an old friend from Snowbird - a guy I worked with on the switchboard all those years ago. He said,

"Remember that girl we worked with? The one you liked? She's back in Utah now too. I saw her not long ago - I have her business card in my car."

That was all I needed to hear. A few minutes later we had her on the phone, and set up a date that evening for a burger and a beer. The reunion was joyous. We all talked for hours, and made up for 28 years of lost time. It was like we hadn't missed a beat. And what I'd liked about her all those years ago? The feelings were still there. The friendship was solid.

She was separated, and at the tail end of a divorce from an unfaithful, mentally abusive man. We started spending every evening together, sitting under the stars, drinking beer, reminiscing, and laughing. During the day, I jumped in and helped her around her house, cooked for her, and tried to make her life nicer. She became re-acquainted with my parents, and helped with my mom occasionally. Our friendship flourished, and after a few months, became romantic. I moved in with her that fall, just as her divorce finalized.

Chapter 24

Off the rails and into Fantasy land

Just because a person is managing his or her recovery, staying on their medication and continuing their therapy, doesn't mean they don't still have their disease. Mine was still there - lurking in the background - it was just managed. Until I made a crucial mistake. I went off my medication.

It wasn't intentional. I got behind on a dose and then tried to play catch up. That made it difficult to sleep, so I didn't take my meds the next day. Before long I was all mixed up and my dark moods began to get the better of me. My behavior started to change. And though I'd successfully

managed my disease for more than 10 years, I
slowly slid off the rails again. Relapse.

Just like with addiction,
when you stop managing
your disease, you're "off the
wagon." It's not uncommon
for bipolar folks to deny they
need their medication. They
start to feel better, decide
they don't need the
medication, stop taking it,
crash and burn. The irony,
and painfully obvious point,
is that the medication was
helping them feel better in
the first place. It's like a
game of Russian Roulette to

suddenly stop your medication. Unpleasant side effects? Discuss them with your doctor. Perhaps your dosage can be tweaked. But don't go off your medication without the consent and oversight of your medical professional.

Timing is everything. And mine couldn't have been worse. In the midst of my vacation from my meds I had a phone call. Remember that crazy girl from my past? The one from high school who came to Texas and tried to convince me to leave my girlfriend? The one who couldn't even take care of herself? Guess who was visiting Salt Lake City?

As I've said so many times before in this story, I'm not proud of what I did next. But this crazy girl was like a siren to a lost fisherman. When we met up, she told me she missed me, and understood my illness better than anyone, and that she'd be the best partner for me. She also needed saving - she had health problems, work problems, her mother was dying, you name it, and for some reason I thought I could help. To my unmedicated brain this all made sense on some level. I took the bait, slept with her, and began an affair. She was the crazy yin to my crazy yang. She fed my full-blown delusions of grandeur. While manic, we made elaborate plans about where we'd go and things we'd do. We fantasized about having tremendous amounts of money and how we'd spend it. It was all ridiculous, but at the time I thought it was real.

> Why did I make this
> completely asinine mistake
> *again*? Well, my 'oyster'
> tells me "if you didn't learn
> your lesson the first time, the
> universe is going to slap ya
> with it again!" WHAM.

Before too long my new girlfriend caught on and kicked me out of the house. What a wakeup call. The fog lifted, I got back on my meds, and I saw the crazy girl for who she was. Shit! What had I done?

When you're clear-minded
for so long and jump ship,
the riptide sweeps you out so
swiftly, and so much further
than you've been before, that
it's difficult to imagine
coming back. Once I was
neck deep in my affair, it
seemed easier to live in a
false fantasy than confront
what my true self knew to be
right. There are reasons
professionals recommend no
relationships while new to
recovery.

A month or so had passed when I looked up,
one day, to see my ex-girlfriend walking through

the door. She was returning a few of my belongings that were left at her house. To be honest I was stunned - I never thought I'd see her again. And worse, if I never saw her again, I *knew* I deserved it. What I had done was despicable. And I should have known better - I had fallen into that trap once before!

With this tiny crack in the door, I made my apologies. I explained I'd been off my meds. I took accountability. I came clean on all the lies. I told her I loved her and that she deserved only the very best of me. Over time, I worked my way back into her good graces, and she took me back. Thank God. I have not been off my meds since - it's not worth the chance.

This is a shout out for those readers who are dealing with a friend or loved one with bipolar. I have four pointers for ail, 1) Set boundaries early, 2) Know your limitations, 3) Expect to have to reconstruct connections, and 4) Accept support from outside sources (friends, family members, or a counselor for yourself). You are inadvertently affected by this disease too.

Mom and dad eventually moved to an assisted living so that mom could have full-time professional care on a Memory Care unit. Dad had an apartment in the same building so they could eat all their meals together, and spend time during the day. It was a tough transition but a necessary one.

She died less than a year later from complications of her illness. Her steep decline happened during her last two weeks. When things took a turn for the worse, my dad reached out to my sister, the doctor, who dropped everything and arrived a few hours later. Mom's sight was gone, she couldn't speak, and she suffered pain, no one could really explain. Two days later, with my father, sister, my girlfriend, and me by her side, my mom passed away gently, quietly, and with dignity. While I would never have wished my mother's death, it was an odd relief to know she was now free of her horrible, unfair, debilitating disease.

I entirely believe, with every fiber of my being, that my reaction to losing my mother would have been drastically different if I were not caring for my own mental well-being. Honestly, it scares me to imagine what it could have been like. Perhaps, and this is easy for me to sell to myself knowing my past, it could have killed me. My mental health regimen saved me this time; not my army buddies, my parents, or hospital personnel. I'm proud of myself for this.

Here's the lesson I learned from my mother's death. Appreciate your moment. Every moment. Make the most of what you have. I was ready to give up my life twice. But facing the death of someone I loved so dearly changed things for me. I realized, in a profound way, that each of us has a purpose, and are needed here. We should fight to the last breath, with dignity, just like my mother did.

Chapter 25
Oyster Too, Delicious Stew

Being a disabled vet entitles me to medical and psychiatric care from the Veteran's Administration (V.A.) Hospital system. As any vet will tell you, treatment at the V. A. can be really hit and miss. And because the Salt Lake V.A. is adjacent to the University of Utah (with a top-notch med school) they get their share of new doctors doing short stints. For many, many years, my primary care doc at the V.A. was never the same person twice. That's bad for a lot of reasons (mostly because there's no consistency for patients) but if you're a psych patient the problem is REALLY magnified. Imagine my frustration, for instance, at having to start over, and explain *my* psych history from the beginning, to a new doc, *every single time* I needed a prescription refilled. It was outrageous. It shouldn't be tolerated; we owe our vets better - especially the crazy ones (and there are more than a few).

I'd been assigned to yet another psychiatrist, and I was fed up. I went in to the appointment and, as could have been predicted, the poor guy asked for my history. Exasperated, I came a little unglued and asked why it mattered, since I'd never see him again, and couldn't he just please fill my prescription so we could both be done with this charade and get on with our day?

But wonder of all wonders - this doctor was different! He seemed to really take to heart what I said, and committed to me, right then and there, that as long as he was at the V.A., he'd be my doctor. He further said he was sorry the V.A. had wasted my time in the past, and that he looked forward to a long relationship with me. Wait, what?

To my amazement, it didn't stop there. A few visits in, this doctor said he thought I'd benefit from some talk therapy. There was a male psych nurse he said, just one office over, who was amazing and really benefiting some of his other patients. The doc said he didn't offer this option to many people. I was super hesitant - honestly, for the same reasons I'd made my initial spiel. Did I really want to start over, again, and tell my history to someone new? No, I decided. I didn't. But the doc persisted so I said I'd give it one shot (just to shut him up).

Consistency is key with your mental health. Try to find a doctor and therapist (and regimen) you like and stay with it. As my story illustrates, it's not always easy. Over the years, depending on whether I've had a job with insurance, I've bounced between private care and the V.A. And while I'm not ungrateful for anyone who had their door open to me when I needed it, I *do* feel the government system is monumentally flawed. I have to wonder if having brand new doctors treating vets is the best approach - I mean, I'd sometimes be seen by doctors that were mere kids, fresh out of college, who often knew much less about my disorder than I did. What's the answer? Again, consistency. How do we get there? Good question.

Reluctantly, I went to see that psych nurse. It was anything but a waste of time. This man was an absolute Godsend, who from the first visit established a relationship with me and showed me his wisdom, just as my therapist in Dallas had done so many years earlier. As we got into it, I realized

I'd forgotten how good this was for me - how beneficial it was on so many levels.

My new 'Oyster' is an honest-to-God groovy man, a student of moods, with a tie-dye shirt and love-em-all personality. He surrounds himself with beautiful things: geodes, feathers, and other natural mood boosters. His psychedelic office is a sanctuary of sorts where I continue to better understand myself and my disease, and have thought provoking breakthroughs. Who's the real oyster here? Does my therapist hold the shiny pearl of answers, or is it me and my original grain of sand, which began as a foreign pain and evolved into a smoothly molded sphere of internal enlightenment? Of strength? Seafood for thought . . .

Own your success in therapy; don't lay it in the lap of your professional. Try not to give as much weight to the personal relationship with your therapist as what they teach you. Listen. Take notes. Do your homework. Knowledge is power; you can take that knowledge and apply it to your life. Defend your regimen, defend your clarity, and most of all, always fight to be better than the hand you've been dealt. No one is responsible for your survival but you. You're the one who walked into a help center in the first place. Take ownership.

Once you've balanced your therapy appointments and your personal life, don't stop there! Participation in outside groups can also be highly beneficial. The more people you allow into your healing process, the more successful it will be. Depression and Bipolar Support Alliance (DBSA) and The National Alliance on Mental Illness (NAMI) are a couple of worthwhile programs. See if there's a regular group meeting in your community.

The most important thing to know about group meetings is that some of the topics might stir you or even trigger you. If you find yourself on edge or out of place, try again another time. If there's a topic you're not comfortable sharing in a group setting, take it to your personal therapist and work it out there. The primary advantage to a group setting is the concept of ideas. They can percolate long after a meeting, which means it's working.

Chapter 26

This is MY soapbox. Stand down.

I get a lot of push back on my ideas - especially from people who don't entirely understand my sense of humor. But with my past, I've *got* to have a sense of humor or I'd be dead.

Spirituality is a sensitive topic but for me, it's a tool in my recovery arsenal. Ever since I was a little kid, being forced to church in dad's blue LTD, I had a relationship with God - just not the way everyone else did.

And when I committed suicide in the Army, and saw the white light, I knew God was there waiting for me. When I held the pistol to my head in Colorado Springs, and the Devil sat there in the same room, waiting, and taunting me, I told him he couldn't have me.   I knew I was God's.

When I became close to the lady with brain cancer at my church, and directed her to look within *herself* for God, I was sharing something I KNEW to be true, to the very depths of my being, though no one had told me the rules. What a gift to know I helped that lady find peace prior to her death.

I reached out to God through Baptism (on more than one occasion), when organized religion told me my illness was my fault. It didn't work - my take away was that God didn't really think that either. He knows I'm mentally ill.

Call me crazy (that's a joke), but MY God has always been there, and MY God has always protected me - and I know I'm going back to MY God when I finally do die, so I'm not afraid of death. I talk to God pretty much every day. God and I are tight.

That's not to say I don't appreciate everyone else's God, because I think it's all ONE God. So, I can appreciate others' religions now more now than ever. If your God and your religion are what holds you together, that's great. And it's your business. You do you.

What I can't condone, however, is ANY established religion placing the blame for mental health disorders on the shoulders of the people suffering from those conditions. Nope. Bullshit. I won't accept that and neither should you.

And one other VERY important point. If you're bipolar, know someone who is, or hold a position in the clergy, please let's not condone the notion that walking through the doors of a church, or performing a ritual (a.k.a. baptism) will cure your mental illness. Plainly stated, it won't. You'll manage your mental illness with the four pillars of medication, therapy, support and sleep. And if you want to have your own daily dialogue with God through prayer, you absolutely should. But if your religion is telling you they'll cure your mental illness, do yourself and them a favor and walk out that door.

This is NOT to bash religion. If your religion floats your boat, and boosts you up, and fills a void in your life, and brings you closer to God, by all means practice your beliefs. I believe there's value, and something to be gained, from all religious traditions. The older I get, and the more I study, the more sense they ALL make, and the more I see that we're more alike than different. The bottom line, don't place all the responsibility for your mental health recovery on the steeple of your church.

Chapter 27
What now?

Today I not only survive, but I truly try to enjoy my life and give back. In addition to working toward a college degree in Social work, I've trained as a Peer Support Mentor at the V.A., lectured, been active in my local DBSA chapter, reached out to people I see who are struggling, and try to be a vocal and visible advocate for the mental health community. I'll talk with anyone who will listen.

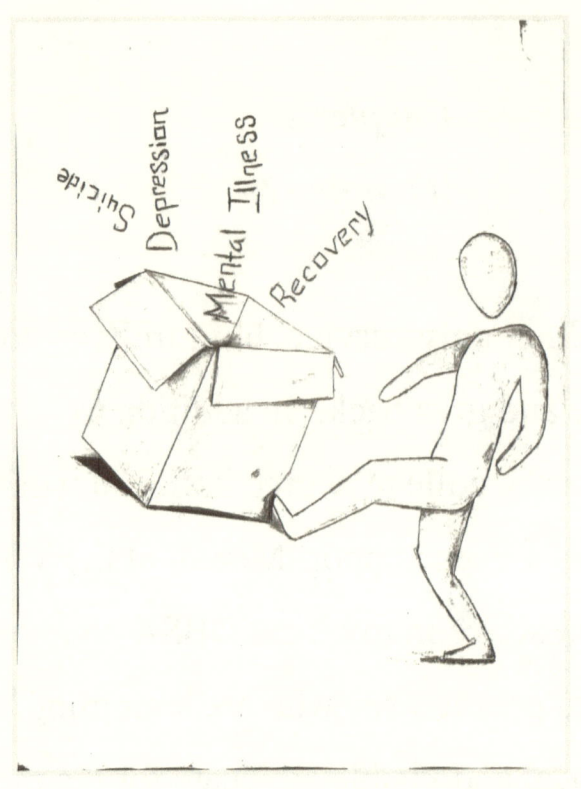

My work is intended to open a dialogue so that, together, we can start waging a war on mental health, and kick this box of fear, shame, and societal stigma to the curb. The box holds everything that's been hidden. Things that couldn't be discussed, like suicide and depression, but also the *hope* for recovery. It's there for all of us, because we ALL know someone with mental illness. Are you ready to do your part and kick the box with me?

Personally, I've come a long way. But that doesn't mean my life is perfect. I still have bad days, screw up, forget my medication here and there, and act - well, human. I've swallowed so much pride that I jokingly tell people I've started to enjoy the taste of it. But that's okay. Because I'm bipolar, which adds a few additional challenges to my daily plate.

Now eighteen years into my recovery, I take each day at a time, try to see my blessings daily, do one or two things I enjoy (like cook a great meal) and appreciate what's important - namely the people in my life and my four cherished dogs (all misfit rescues). I'm still learning. I'm not happy every day, and that's okay. My goal is more happy days than not. My inevitable mood swings are not as deep or long as they used to be; yes, I still have them - I just understand them better now, and better know how to take care of myself when they happen. Thinking back on all the sweet wishes my mother expressed for me as a new baby, I think she'd approve of the person I've become.

Considering I went so long without an intervention, diagnosis or treatment, it's a miracle I am even alive. I've come to one grand conclusion: that <u>God must have me here, and sharing this story, for a reason!</u>

Art speaks to the bipolar affective disorder mind, and of the 2.8% of the world population who are bipolar, a large percentage are "artists" in their own right (painters, illustrators, sculptors, actors, comedians, chefs, musicians, and the like). Why? Because a lot of emotions that are difficult to explain are easier to represent in an image. It's a piece of heart and mind you can see and feel in your own way, at your own discretion. Also, when a bipolar person is focusing on their craft they are in a good space - immersed in something wonderful. When they're outside of their craft

they have problems. My art is
cooking, and the place I find
solace is the kitchen. Encourage
more art; it's good for everyone!

Maybe the reason is giving hope to even one
person struggling with a mental illness that there IS
light at the end of the tunnel. There is hope. You
just have to keep going and keep looking until you
find it.

Maybe it's to help people with mental illness
forgive themselves for all the bad shit they did
when they were unwell and unmedicated. Hey, you
couldn't help it. We could all stand to give each
other a little grace. Lord knows I had to forgive
myself before I could start getting better.

Maybe it's to illustrate (ever so graphically) to a spouse, sibling, or parent of a mentally ill loved one, that their family member's strange or erratic behavior is typical for someone with their disease. They need support, understanding, diagnosis, medication, and therapy. But above all, they need their family's unwavering love.

Maybe it's to show that you shouldn't ever give up on a person. Don't give up on your sick family member. Don't give up on yourself. Look at the trials I endured; if I can get through it, so can you.

Maybe it's to encourage one person to reach out to a person they know who may be struggling, to just say hello, lend an ear, and ask how they're doing?

Maybe it's to educate society that mental illness is not something the sufferers choose. They didn't choose it any more than someone chooses cancer or diabetes. It's a disease. And with proper care and treatment, the mentally ill (just like the physically ill) can live wonderful, full lives.

Maybe it's to free one person from the bondage of a religious tradition that tells them that their affliction is their fault.

Maybe it's to give one person the hope they need not to commit suicide.

Maybe it's to open conversations about mental illness, and make it something that people can openly talk about, and freely admit, without embarrassment or fear of stigma.

Maybe it's to illustrate to the government that more money needs to be spent on mental health care - not only at the community level, but for our vets.

Maybe it will help a parent recognize a behavior of mental illness in their child, and have the child evaluated early.

Maybe it's so one more person can admit to their co-workers or boss that they're struggling, without having to worry they'll lose their job.

Maybe it's to show someone with mental illness that they're not alone - there's others of us out there, lots of us, and we SEE you, FEEL your pain, and want the best for you.

Maybe it's so we can ALL kick this big box of mental illness stigma, and send it flying.

Maybe it's so we can all help Just One person. How amazingly different would the world be if everyone committed to helping Just One?

Maybe, it's all of the above. I hope that's the case. Because, my friends, we need change. Together, with everyone's help, we can win this war, and quit sweeping mental illness under the rug.

###

www.ingramcontent.com/pod-product-compliance
Lightning Source LLC
Chambersburg PA
CBHW020314290526
45785CB00007B/2794